The Making of Design

Gerrit Terstiege (Ed.)

The Making of Design

From the First Model
to the Final Product

Birkhäuser
Basel · Boston · Berlin

Chairs 25

Interiors 67

Transportations 117

Experiments 141

Models with a Cause

If shape is the opposite of "matter", then there is no design that can be called "material": It is always informative. And if shape is the "how" of matter, and "matter" the "what" of shape, then design is one of the methods of giving matter shape and making it look thus, and not different.
Vilém Flusser, "Form und Material", Vienna, 1991

_____The look behind the scenes, which we are daring to take here, illustrates the erroneous, errant and roundabout paths designers took before coming up with shapes that subsequently seem to be so obvious and self-evident. When presented, perfectly lit and brand new in showrooms, displays, and shelves there is not a single trace of the effort that went into their creation. However, any designer familiar with the doubts, and setbacks that go with any creative process, will very much appreciate the work of their colleagues who, on the following pages, grant an insight into their projects. Design, as becomes clear in every single one of these process reports, is concerned with details, proportions and perforations, combining materials and subtle finishes. Methods and strategies can accompany and steer this process, but no more – they cannot necessarily make it any faster. Perhaps it is comforting for some of them to see that even such experienced designers as Ronan and Erwan Bouroullec had to conduct numerous studies before coming up with the ultimate shape of the Vegetal Chair: a whole four years of development were needed before they and their partners at Vitra were convinced by the result. The magazine form was the very first publication to feature the Vegetal Chair's design process. The same applies to many other products, i.e. Konstantin Grcic's cantilever chair MYTO, which was included in the MoMA design collection practically straight from the factory.
_____ In the sense of Flusser, the material in this book, its form and its content, is intended to be informative: After all, it collates a selection of the

best design process reports, which have been a firm feature of the magazine form since 2006. It is not without reason that the claim of the magazine has been chosen as the title of this compendium: The Making of Design. Without the protagonists being prepared to open up, to expose design steps, it would have been inconceivable. Of course the extent to which alterations to a model might be staged as "nice mistakes", while much from the bumpy initial phase of a project is kept quiet about, cannot always be checked. But that is, as it were, in the nature of things. Nowadays, in the movie industry, "making of" features, in other words commentaries by actors and directors together with outtakes, stunts and dialogs gone wrong are now part and parcel of the marketing chain of major Hollywood productions. With regards to design, a background report of this nature can be hampered or even prevented by several factors: The client company can oppose the publication of sensitive information, the designer might not have had any decent photos made during the design process, models and sketches were not archived and simply thrown away …

_____ Without doubt, also the journalistic preparation of design studies using photos, drawings, renderings and prototypes is a process that can also go wrong. That this was not so in the case of these essays I would like to thank the renowned authors such as Andrea Eschbach, Karianne Fogelberg, Kristina Raderschad and Oliver Herwig, my colleagues Katharina Altemeier, Karen Bofinger, as well as Markus Zehentbauer, who, as our Chief Text Editor, edited a great number of these essays. My thanks also go to Silja van der Does, who as Art Director of form was not only responsible for the layout of many features in the magazine, but also came up with the design of the book. My great thanks go to all of them – and of course not least to the designers and photographers who were willing to take us on the at times adventurous journey from the first model to the final product.

_____ Gerrit Terstiege

Dieter Rams: "The Design Process Still had no Form"

The long-standing chief designer at Braun, Dieter Rams, talks about the development of the Kronberg-based company's design processes. The interview was conducted by Gerrit Terstiege in February 2009.

Terstiege Since 2006, form magazine has reported in detail on the development of the design of current products – and it is hard to conceive of such processes today without thinking of computers. Looking back, do you regret working as a designer at a time when computers did not have the possibilities they offer today?

Rams ___ Yes and no. Of course, computers make working as a team in a network far easier these days. Yet on the other hand people often get up to a lot of mischief with computer renderings and they sugarcoat problematic areas wonderfully. I have always loathed renderings and regularly fought against them. My drawings and sketches were generally intuitively to scale and, even if they were really abstract, the team of model builders was able to make them without any problem. Although they were less set-in-stone, less precise, they showed exactly what I wanted. I worked a great deal with sketches.

Terstiege How did you actually find your own particular drawing style, characterized by a great simplicity?

Rams ___ I had a good drawing teacher at my school, the Werkkunstschule in Wiesbaden, his name was Mr. Rotfuchs. He taught illustration, and we aspiring architects regularly had to practice figurative drawing. When I started cross-hatching, as everyone does when they try out freehand drawing for the first time, Mr. Rotfuchs said to me: "Forget that nonsense, you just need to make the line a bit thicker, you can achieve spatiality that way, too!" Essentially my mode of representation culminates in as simple a line drawing as possible.

Terstiege New products are generally created in and by a team; at the end of the day design and technology must go hand in hand. How was the development process at Braun structured under your direction? How did you proceed when you had to find a new form for a particular device?

Rams ___ When I think back to my early years at Braun, in the mid-1950s, I remember lots of problems resulting from insufficient cooperation between designers and engineers. Back then, we first had to explore and develop the types and means of cooperation.

Terstiege Can you give me an example?

Dieter Rams, born in 1932 in Wiesbaden, was chief designer at Braun from 1961 until 1995. His multi-award-winning designs have influenced generations of designers and been the subject of international exhibitions and publications. He lives in Kronberg near Frankfurt, Germany.

Editor Gerrit Terstiege, who first interviewed Rams in 1997 while still studying design, in the studio of Rams' house.

Rams ___ For example when Hans Gugelot from the Hochschule für Gestaltung Ulm was at the Braun plant in Frankfurt, he spoke to brothers Erwin and Arthur Braun, the company owners, and Dr. Eichler, who was responsible for the company's design-strategic orientation. Thus Hans Gugelot discussed issues on a level which had nothing to do with the technical side of product development. This could only work as long as all that was required was pure redesign: giving existing technology a makeover. And as we all know, that was not what Gugelot had in mind. He wanted to beat a completely new path. He was not happy that the exterior of these first devices he repackaged promised more than the interior delivered. This deficit had to be corrected. Erwin Braun quickly realized that design at Braun had to take place in house.

Terstiege That must have been a decisive point for you, 1955, since Braun originally hired you as an architect and interior designer not a product designer.

Rams ___ That's right. It soon came about that one of my tasks in the design department was to harmonize the relationship between the designers and engineers, to build trust. To an extent, the design process still had no form then. For example, there was no briefing. Later we formed teams, consisting of designers, marketing people and engineers, who worked together on a product right from the start. Overall conditions like these have a tremendous effect on the design process. The design projects then followed the tasks set by the relevant business areas, i.e., hi-fi, body care, healthcare etc. There was a business director, who was on equal footing with the technical director and design director. I was the only one, thank God, who reported directly to the CEO. That helped a great deal. My successor's situation was different, by the way.

Terstiege BWhen did these structures really establish themselves at Braun?

Rams ___ That was in the course of the 1970s. It was necessary, owing to continually increasing sales, to design for international markets and also to always work on a number of different projects simultaneously. You could say that what we now call globalization started very early at Braun. Also with the help of Gillette AG, which had taken over Braun in 1967.

Terstiege Is there a product that proved to be a particular headache for you in organizing its development?

Rams ___ Yes, that would have to be the Atelier system, which would become the "last edition", and which heralded the end of the hi-fi era at Braun. I visited our engineers in Japan several times, because a number of Japanese companies fitted the Atelier components with the corresponding electronic internals. The tuner came from one company, the amplifier from another, the technology for the record player from yet another. Fortunately they were all based in Tokyo, but I couldn't see everything fitting together at the end. Some of the Japanese firms, in turn, had part produced in Singapore, which didn't make things easier. But in the end it all came together.

Dieter Rams and Terstiege in conversation. The stereo, the table and the table lamp shown here were designed or at least co-designed by Rams. This also holds true for many of the objects in his house.

Terstiege And in the mid-1950s, when Braun design was taking shape, were there no structures or guidelines for the design process?

Rams ___ Back then there was quite simply no definable design process. A great deal was created based on emotion, the result of certain facts, including a consideration of what was actually possible in terms of production etc. An idea came from here, and one from there. Personally I always acknowledged the value of technical innovations suggested by my team.

Terstiege The word emotion is surprising in this context. So how is it the decision came to be made in the early 1960s to create such a complex and costly device as the T1000 multi-band radio? I bet that wasn't based on a gut feeling?

Rams ___ On the one hand the first small portable radios very quickly faced competition: the Japanese rapidly adapted the transistor technology and then launched similar-sized radios onto the market at half the price. We couldn't beat that. Yet on the other hand the transistor technology offered possibilities we wanted to make use of. So we decided to make a multi-band radio with a build quality and features that could not be copied so easily. Considerations such as these definitely played a role, but the strategies of marketing teams didn't. Incidentally, when marketing started to rule the roost at Olivetti in the late 1970s, Ettore Sottsass quit the company and turned his attention to creating free designs and experiments. And that then led to the foundation of Memphis. However, this step was easier for

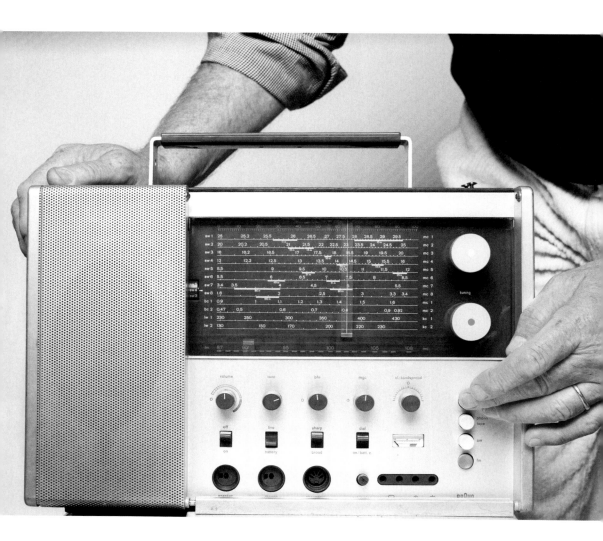

him, because he was never what one might call a permanent employee at Olivetti. My situation was quite different.

Terstiege At that time, around 1980, you had been employed at Braun for 25 years and were heading a large team as chief designer. And we can't imagine you suddenly leaving to paint vases and exhibit them in galleries… But how was it that marketing at Braun was able to gain such an influence? After all, you and your design team had shown that you could create outstanding products without input from the marketing department.

Rams ___ It had to do with the ever-larger quantities we had to produce. And following on from that, that a more complex production technique also requires big investments in tool making and production facilities. In the late 1970s, marketing had more influence because it was its responsibility to ensure competitiveness and a return on investment.

The Beatles' LP "Abbey Road" rotates on the 1962 record player called PCS5. Left page: Rams with the T1000 world receiver he designed for Braun.

Terstiege Marketing people started paying more attention to what the competition was doing.

Rams ___ Not only that. Innovations in design and technology suddenly had a more difficult time of it, because they always involve risks, including precisely economic risks. Without fully automated production there came a point when things simply couldn't go on, because without it you couldn't produce the expected quantities. Huge production facilities like these were masterpieces in themselves, but they were just so investment intensive that the question increasingly loomed: when will we get back the money we invested in this or that facility? As a consequence, we were increasingly reluctant to give new ideas the green light.

Terstiege A huge number of photos and drawings have appeared in recent years of Braun products that were never realized. This was how, decades later, we learnt of the concept of a portable television from the early 1960s which was related to the T1000. Why did it never see the light of day?

Rams ___ Here too, the general consensus was that we would not be able to sell enough of those small televisions. Brionvega and others later showed that portable televisions can be a great success on the market. Yet perhaps

Opposite page: Today, this Braun SK4, better known as "Snow White's Coffin", stands in Dieter Rams' basement workshop. The black-and-white photograph on the wall was taken by his wife Ingeborg who was employed as a photographer at Braun.

this is precisely the reason for the current problems: no-one wants to admit that at a certain point they have reached the end of the line. You can't always make yet another new shaver, yet another new coffee machine without there really being something new about it – except a slight change in form or a different color. And then you think you can further increase sales with it. It's an illusion! But obviously, most managers still seem to believe that it's just the sheer volume of products sold that counts. The automobile industry is currently experiencing the same problem: For years, the car manufacturers' goal has been to push ever-more cars onto the market, when it's obvious that there are too many cars, that the markets have long been saturated. Yet it is precisely objectives like these that still shape the design process in the design departments of major companies today. But I am sticking with my maxim: Less, but better – that's the way.

_____ www.braun.com
_____ www.sdr-plus.com
_____ www.vitsoe.com
_____ Fotos: www.dieterschwer.com

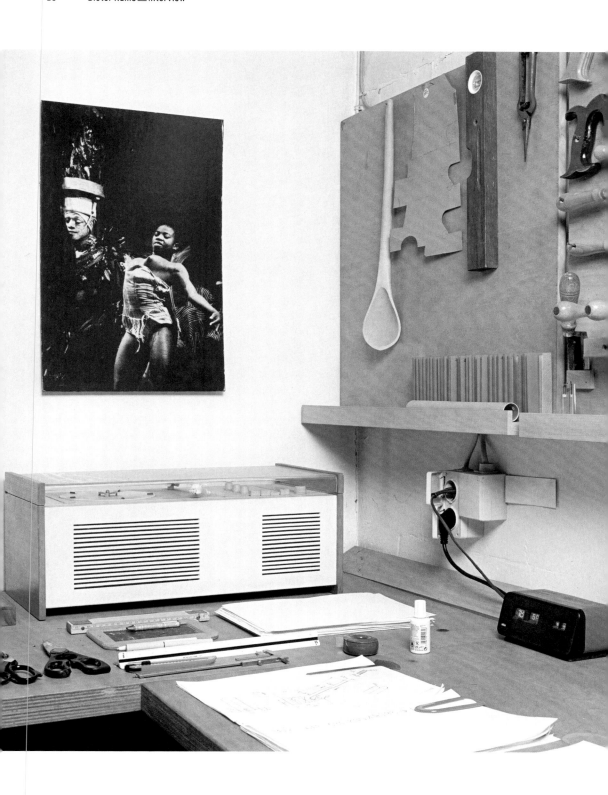

Konstantin Grcic: "The Beauty of Paper is Dangerous"

Terstiege Few people know that you created the shapes of your most famous designs almost exclusively using paper, scissors, scalpel and adhesive tape. I would be interested to know whether you resort to the simple material of paper because it essentially suits your design language or is it even the case that paper influences the final shape of your products?

Grcic ____ I am quite sure that relying on paper models for so many years has influenced my design language. It is not necessarily a conscious thing – but I am always open to it happening. Paper simply offers me the means of working three-dimensionally very quickly on a 1:1 scale. You could say they are 3D sketches. And, just as it is easy to rework certain parts of a pencil sketch, it is easy to make alterations to paper. We build these models, destroy them again, replace parts and so on. After all, they are not meant for presentation, but are working tools intended to achieve an initial result quickly. At any rate, paper fits wonderfully into our work: we can realize everything ourselves on the spot in the office, which means we are not reliant on an external workshop at an early design stage.

Terstiege But you do not manage entirely without a computer, do you?

Grcic ____ No, in fact we even start out with a rough digital rendering. We then use Rhinoceros to generate a version of the surface, after which we build the first paper model. Next we check the result, make some modifications, and then go back to the computer to record these steps. After which the computer gives us another variation from which to make another model and so on.

Terstiege In other words, there is a constant interplay between traditional and digital renderings. But don't you limit yourself by opting to use paper for model building? After all, it is not possible to make all the shapes you could create with great precision through hard foam milling or laser sintering.

Grcic ____ Yes, you could certainly describe that as limiting yourself. Though we always have the option of moving on to more complex shapes. But the limitations paper imposes also help you not to waste time on unimportant details. It speeds up decision making, quite irrespective of whether you are dealing with a chair or a kitchen appliance. The tasks are always the same, designing something, evolving the statics and volumes of a product, inte-grating technical components or finding the ideal shape for a seat pan. And paper models are simply ideal for all of these things. But sometimes you experience real surprises when using paper and cardboard for design. Take the Mars chair that Classicon manufactures. First of all, we created a very rough version of it with cardboard and tape. I just wanted to visualize the

Konstantin Grcic prefers to work with paper models – he says the material influences his formal language.

Inspite of Grcic´s prefer-ence, sometimes paper is simply not stable enough a material. On the left is a fragile paper model of the "Tin" stool, the other images show the prelim. studies for "Chair One", which Grcic designed in 2003, again for Magis.

surfaces and geometry. It was to be upholstered. Initially I conceived it as a very soft chair. But at some point the shape of the cardboard model was suddenly so powerful that we wanted to retain it. The upholsterer from Classicon encouraged us to just put a soft cover over a hard shape, and he created a pattern for it. In this instance you really can say that the material of the model, and the way we handled it determined the final design.

Terstiege But if you can't get any further with paper and cardboard, you do resort to other model building materials, don't you?

Grcic _____ Quite right. When we developed the kitchen appliances for Krups there came a point where we knew we couldn't continue using cardboard. In such cases we turn to the computer. Or we employ other materials – clay, plaster or even plasticine.

Terstiege How was it for exmaple with Square, your first wastepaper basket for Authentics, whose form gradually alters from a circle at its base to a square at the upper rim. Is it possible to achieve a subtle shape like that by just using paper?

Grcic _____ No, it's not. But I always build three-dimensional models, because there are many things I can't judge from a drawing or a computer rendering. However, in the case of Square the model was also really simple: It was made completely of wire, and I used a kind of 3D drawing: it followed the circular shape of the base, then formed a vertical line that defined the cut out handle and the basket's height, finishing in a square. And we solely used a paper model to design the waste bin Tip some years ago. We built fully working models of that in paper, complete with hinging mechanism and everything that goes with it.

Terstiege You have emphasized the speed with which you can visualize volumes and proportions. As such your paper models could also be described as "rapid prototypes". But isn't foaming a much quicker method of achieving what you want? You just take a big block of foam, push the button and in a matter of minutes you can take a look at the result.

Grcic defines the volume and proportions using a stable life-size model made of paper and card. Left: Two studies for the shape of "Mars", a Classicon chair, above a model of the Chaos sofa for Classicon.

Grcic _____ I have a strong dislike of foaming models. They just produce dirt, this really fine dust everywhere. I don't want that in the studio. That aside, it's easier to make modifications in paper, to add sections or remove them. Removing things is really easy with foam. But then rebuilding it again is awfully complicated, you have to use adhesive again, and it doesn't dry properly. Or the new element you have stuck on falls off again. Stuff like that is really annoying.

From espresso machine to mixer: Grcici also started out with paper models for his kitchen appliances designed for Krups.

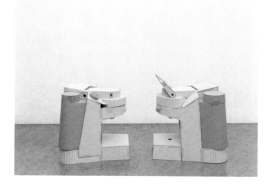

Terstiege Of course there are designers who not only used paper and cardboard to build models but actually employed it to create products – I am thinking of the famous folding furniture by Peter Raacke, at the end of the 1960s. Raacke imagined products that could easily be put together, that were light and affordable. Of course, his chairs and sofas didn't last long. But still, does that idea attract you, too? After all, you really can sit on the cardboard model of your Chaos Sofa ...

Grcic That sort of thing has never interested me. If you start to work with insertions, folding and reinforcements everything is suddenly so ingenious. Not that I wish to belittle Raacke's cardboard furniture. It was the product of a certain era, and some of the things were intended for children and were really not that bad. What I find really brilliant is Frank O. Gehry's cardboard armchair Beaver that he designed during a Vitra workshop.

Terstiege Photographer Thomas Demand destroys his worlds of paper once he has photographed them. You actually archive your models. Why is that?

Grcic Sometimes I hold on to them in the same way you might keep a beautiful pencil drawing. Perhaps there really is an element of sentimentality. But you have to be careful: The beauty of paper is dangerous at the point where you fall prey to it during your work. You always have to be willing to make hard cuts. But these cuts are themselves great illustrations of the design process. Which is why they still mean so much to me years later.

_____ www.konstantin-grcic.com
_____ www.authentics.de
_____ www.classicon.com
_____ www.krups.com
_____ Fotos: www.dieterschwer.com

Born in 1966, Konstantin Grcic is one of the most influential contemporary designers. He studied at London's Royal College of Art, was an assistant to Jasper Morrison and today heads his own studio KGID in Munich, Germany. He has received commissions from companies such as Flos, Authentics, Magis, Moormann, Classicon, Krups and Plank. The MoMA in New York has included a number of Grcic's designs in its permanent collection.

Chairs

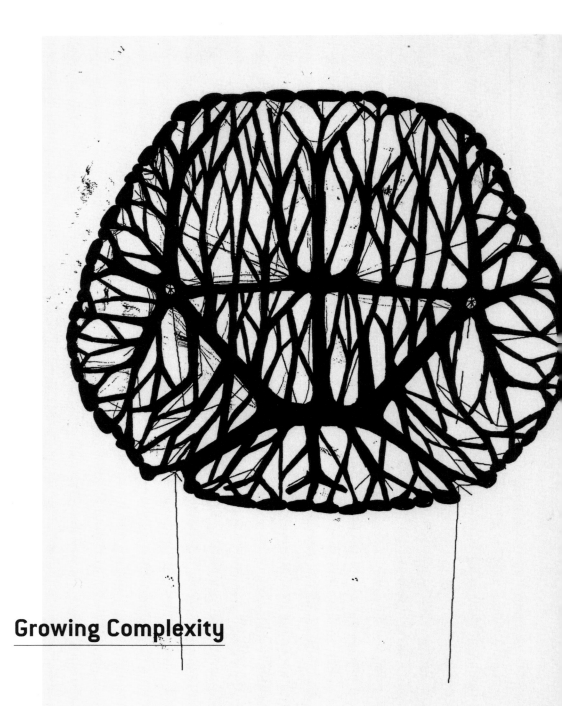

Growing Complexity

Ronan and Erwan Bouroullec spent four years working on a chair whose structure is derived from the growth of plants. The Vegetal Chair, produced by Vitra, was presented at the Milan Furniture Fair 2009. But how did the Bouroullec brothers develop its unique structure?

_____ Can you plant a chair? You can. In 19th century North America young trees were shaped over the course of several years until they adopted the contours of a chair. Ronan and Erwan Bouroullec were so fascinated by this traditional technique that they came up with the idea of designing a "grown chair." What has to grow needs time, and as such the Vegetal Chair was created via an unusually long design process. About four years after the first idea emerged, the chair of fibre-reinforced polyamide was presented at Milan's furniture fair in 2009. That is truly a long time for a chair. But the result is very special: Elements resembling flat branches extend and interweave into an asymmetrical, irregular seating shell. The woven strips are stabilized by ribs which grow downwards and merge with the legs. Viewed from the rear, the chair looks like a leaf with several stalks and numerous veins branching off. "As designers, it is our task to find new structures, new forms of construction," explains Ronan Bouroullec with regard to his work. "And this chair is primarily structure and not just a mere motif." But how come the Vegetal Chair appears to be anything but an assembled construction, more like a single cast? A second inspiring idea, which was the result of the Bouroullecs'

intensive work with die casting, mingled with the initial idea of the grown chair. "In the die casting process, plastic shoots into the form like blood into veins," says Ronan, "and the finer and more branched the form is, the better the plastic is distributed." The brothers quickly had a clear image in mind. Delicate, round legs growing upwards, bending and branching into a ramified seat surface, meandering up and branching out again into back and armrests. When they first showed their sketchbook full of ideas to Vitra, the response was instantly enthusiastic.

Ronan and Erwan Bouroullec designed the seat of the Vegetal Chair as a mesh. Its modified structure was later transfered into various 3-D models.

_____ Egon Bräuning, Head of Product Development, found the idea "provocative and fresh": "In the early developmental stage the two designers did not explore feasibility as much. You can tell that from the chair." Just a few months after the first meeting the Bouroullecs constructed a 3D model of their chair vision: a chair had emerged that was completely asymmetrical, interwoven, as if nature had actually been the constructor, but which, even

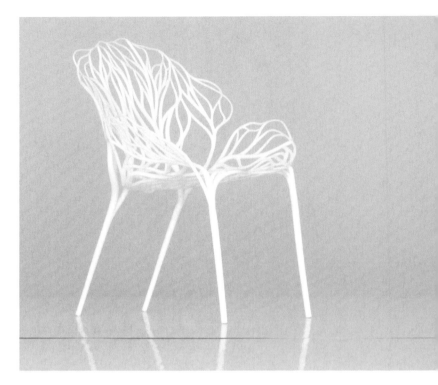

The design process for the Vegetal Chair took almost four years: The first stereo-lithography on a scale of 1:10 looked very different (above). Below: we can see how the structure is trans-fered to a Styrofoam model.

though this did not appear to be the case, could nevertheless be stacked. But it was precisely the technical feasibility which put clear limits on this initial design. It soon became obvious that the veined and branching chair could never be die cast and ejected, nor was there any way of calculating the stability of a completely asymmetrical seat. Nevertheless, the Bouroullec brothers did not let this hinder them, and neither did Egon Bräuning and Vitra Chairman, Rolf Fehlbaum. "At Vitra you feel like you are under a sort of protective cover," says Ronan Bouroullec about the collaboration, laughing. The brothers were to keep working on the project without paying attention to market constraints.

Countless variations of the mesh were created on large strips of paper: however, four points of intersection are marked because of the position of the chair legs.

_____ On the bottom floor of the three-story Paris office, where the furniture workshop is to be found, they now began to play around with various graphic forms. On large sheets of paper the Bouroullecs drew different seat versions, varied the meshwork of the many small branches and compared

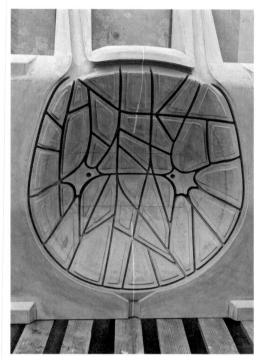

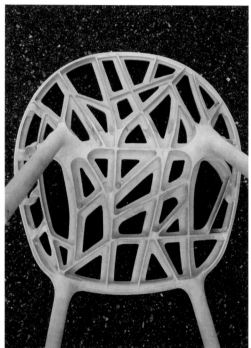

We can clearly make out the deep struts in the cast (top left) — and the two holes for the screws in the back legs, which are only there to increase the pressure on the adhesive. They are not removed later.

From the second to the third dimension and back again: Ronan Bouroullec working on one of the many models of the seat.

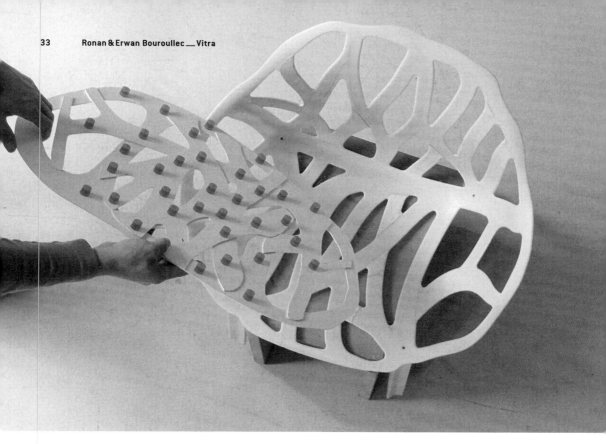

In order to imitate even more closely the complexity of natural branch growth, the brothers placed the structures of several Forex panels on top of each other (right). Later they reduced the number of supports.

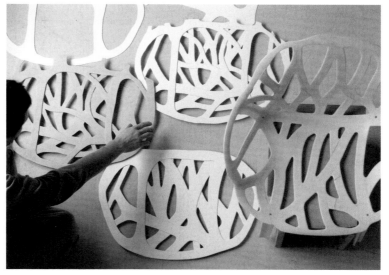

Ronan Bouroullec painted the prototype of the Vegetal Chair himself. The end product, shown on the right, was recently launched in six different colors.

them with other structures composed of fewer, wider branches. With every single pattern they had to make sure they integrated a rectangle of stable supporting elements into the seat, one which visually disappeared into the structure. The seating shell also demanded a stable substructure which would not require too much material. At one of the many regular meetings at Vitra a solution was found in the form of a T-profile. "The T-profile was primarily a rational decision," admits Erwan Bouroullec, "but once we had found the solution things began to flow again."

_____ However, when the first resin model was cast a nasty surprise awaited them. "We sat on the chair and realized that it was anything but comfortable," recalls Erwan Bouroullec. The construction's framework was finished but there was no end in sight to the to-and-fro between ergonomics, design and technical feasibility. How could the seating shell be designed more ergonomically? Why did the seat look more like a perforated surface than branches that have grown together? The brothers made some crucial decisions: they reduced the number of branches and flattened them, thereby improving the ergonomics. To lend the seating shell a grown character the seat was divided into three levels and interwoven at the crossover points. The Bouroullecs cut up innumerable resin models and used modelling clay to arrange them in different forms. "We were constantly building models to help us understand why the chair was so clear in our minds and yet so awful in reality," says Ronan Bouroullec.

_____ The long overlooked problem of the legs was finally confronted. It was suggested by Vitra that they cast the front legs together with the seating shell and keep the back legs separate, glueing them in later. The flow from legs to seating shell had to be worked on in great creative detail. And the hardest part of all was to calculate the dividing line of the two parts of the mould without creating a ridge. Mr. Egon Bräuning who has worked at Vitra for 45 years says "this was the most complicated project I have ever experienced." We believe him.

_____ www.bouroullec.com
_____ www.vitra.com
_____ Text: Miriam Irle

Rococo Rocks!

What did Louis XV have to do with the chemical element manganese? At first sight, zilch. New York architects Benjamin Aranda and Chris Lasch, however, have researched the matter a little more closely and come up with not just a story but an entire chair that combines the structures of Rococo furniture with the crystal lattice of manganese molecules.

_____ It is a moot point whether the objects which are currently on show at collector fairs in London, Basle and Miami and exhibited more as art than design are in fact design at all. The term "design art" introduced by the trade does not help much either. But what is interesting about these limited editions is the direction in which their forms are efflorescing. Crystals – or at least prismatic patterns – have been polished to the point that they truly sparkle, while others have designed extravagant tables and seating such as was last seen in Art Déco or Rococo days. Both reflect the zest for luxury and for the bizarre. At first glance, Aranda/Lasch's Fauteuil Chair, the like of which was last seen at Design Miami in December, brings all this together. It is not entirely coincidental that the piece, composed of crystalline aluminum modules, is reminiscent of a Rococo chair.

_____ Indeed, the New York architects Benjamin Aranda (34) and Chris Lasch (35) had made an in-depth study of Rococo furniture which surrounded Louis XV in his day. "Louis XV established a style that had an appearance of luxury and excess," says Chris Lasch. But what interested the two more was the development of new formal structures: "You can look at an item of Rococo furniture as a structure that is basically as complex as the geometry of a crystal," according to Lasch. The story of the Fauteuil Chair provides the context. Aranda/Lasch discovered that Louis XV died in the very year in which chemist Johan Gottlieb Gahn discovered the element manganese. A seemingly trivial coincidence, and yet one that nevertheless provided the starting point for their concept. They downloaded a mathematical description of a manganese molecule from the Internet, stored the data in their CAD program and calculated a crystal form on the basis of the atomic positions composed of four large hexagons and four smaller triangles as lateral surfaces. Then they proceeded with the aid of algorithms to use the periodic lattice structure of the manganite crystal to generate a chair from 350 identical elements.

_____ The complex part of it was not the individual element, but rather the question of how these various elements could be joined together and how a concrete chair could be formed from the abstract crystal lattice.

Currently, Benjamin Aranda and Chris Lasch can best realize their architectural ideas on the scale of furniture, for example, with the Fauteuil Chair.

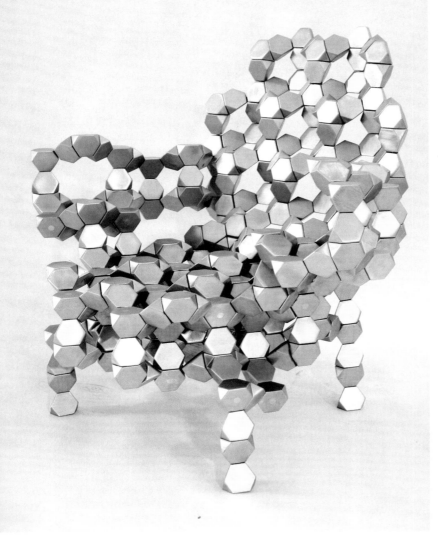

Extravagant Rococo furniture such as this armchair and the chemical element manganese formed the starting points for the design. The designers produced ten specimens from cast aluminum elements for the New York-based gallery owner Paul Johnson.

A chair takes shape: The Fauteuil Chair was created using a three-dimensional lattice structure, from which Aranda and Lasch removed individual elements until they had the shape they wanted. The different shades of color on the screenshot (right) show the 17 possible ways in which the modules can be combined.

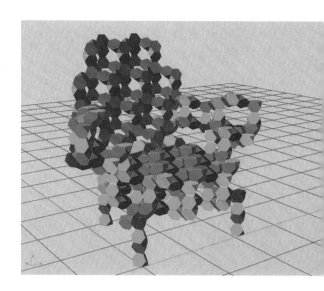

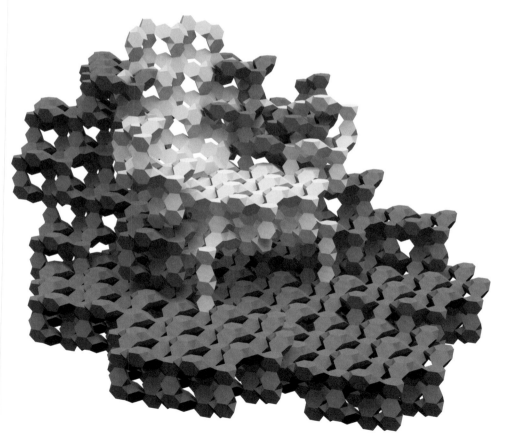

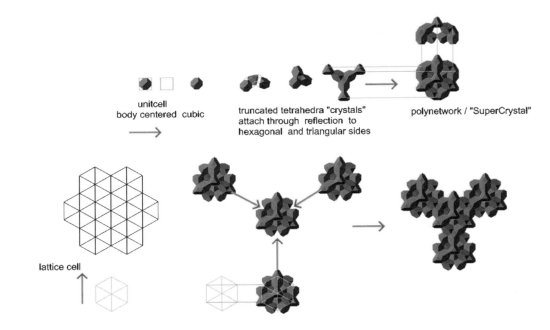

unitcell
body centered cubic

truncated tetrahedra "crystals"
attach through reflection to
hexagonal and triangular sides

polynetwork / "SuperCrystal"

lattice cell

How do manganite mole-
cules behave when they
combine? As the diagram
shows, they form larger elements that can be used in
a modular way just like the
individual elements.

Assistant Clay Coffey trans-
fers the digital template
to the model made of laser-
cut cardboard. He notes
down on tags how many
holes need to be cut in the
individual elements and
how many parts are needed
(left page).

Aranda/Lasch realized that the elements formed rings. "We copied the rings, translated them and moved them throughout the lattice to make a solid packing of rings." Finally they removed as many elements as it took until the silhouette of a chair emerged. You cannot see that the elements are held together with steel pins; there are 17 different possible combination between two or three elements; these were also calculated laboriously on the computer so that no unnecessary holes appeared later on.

_____ The chair will soon be produced in an edition of ten by Baker's Moulds & Patterns. The costs will be paid by New York gallery owner Paul Johnson. Aranda/Lasch have now designed four pieces for him, including a sideboard into which the pattern of ice crystals has been milled. "How many are produced and in what context they are sold is, in a way, beside the point for us," says Lasch. "For us, working on furniture is the opportunity to realize our architectonic ideas, even if it is on a different scale." They have been working for some time now on the idea of combining aperiodic molecular patterns, in other words those which repeat unpredictably, with modularity. This is how they came upon crystal forms and geometries which are particularly suited to this purpose. In 2005, with their most complex project to date Aranda/Lasch reached the final in the competition to design a grotto for the courtyard of P.S.1 in New York. However, the design was never realized. They had planned to put together an aperiodic structure made of four differently formed polyhedrons, modular on the one hand, yet so complex that it would seem to have grown naturally.

_____ Compared with this, the Fauteuil Chair derives from a much simpler system. Nevertheless it makes an impression – as both object and idea. And even though it is created from numerous formulae Lasch finds it important that he is not be confused with a scientist: "The way scientists work is to uncover objective data. We use very similar tools but our end is always subjective. It's always design," says Lasch. The function, however, is not the paramount issue. "You can sit on it," says Lasch, and goes on to report that "we are working on making it more comfortable." Until that fine day arrives, a cushion comes in handy.

_____ www.arandalasch.com
_____ www.johnsontradinggallery.com
_____ Text: Markus Zehentbauer

Steel pins hold the aluminum elements together. To prevent holes and pins being visible on the chair later on, the 17 possible combinations of two or three elements had to be calculated on the computer in what could be called a painstaking process.

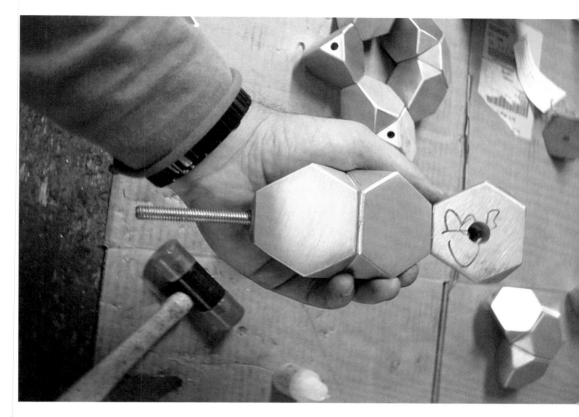

In the Baker's Moulds &Patterns workshop in Canada. The aluminum parts for the Fauteuil Chair are cast here.

Very Round, Indeed

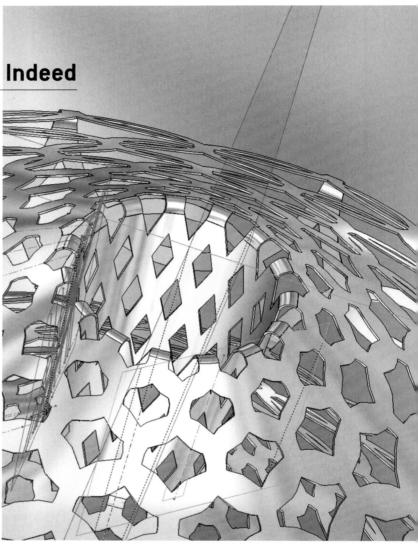

Copenhagen-based designer Louise Campbell used paper, scalpel and sticky tape when creating the Very Round Chair from of 260 circular elements. It is physically strong, yet delicate, and it reinterprets the essence of the chair with playful ease.

_____ Is it still possible to come up with new designs for a classic icon like the chair? An object that has taken on so many forms and expressions over the years? With the Very Round Chair Louise Campbell embarked on this expedition equipped with a strong symbol, the circle. The designer's journey was long, and she had to navigate between hope and despair: will it be strong enough? Will it work? The answer is yes. "There are countless ways of approaching a design. When charged with a given assignment, one works in close collaboration with the client. A number of criteria must be met, and function usually takes priority. Very Round marks a break from this approach," says Louise Campbell. "It stems from my preferred approach, which is completely free from established rules and based instead on sheer playfulness. Initially, most of my design processes are impulsive and inquisitive. With paper, scalpel and sticky tape as my only tools, I cut and unfold the possibilities. And I cut a large number of models. The proportions have to be perfect."

_____ The main emphasis was on the art of simplification. In terms of form, motif and construction Louise Campbell cut to the bone. The Very Round Chair has no legs. No identifiable seat, and no back. The chair is made from one material throughout, a 2-mm steel frame, and the basic form, the circle, was repeated 260 times in order to eventually reappear as a large, welcoming, three-dimensional circle. Deconstructed yet firmly rooted, the Very Round Chair's net of circles is the main construction theme. The structure creates an almost holographic effect, and the shadows perform a circular dance on the floor in an imaginary doubling of the physical shape. "I had to work out the best way to position the circles in relation to each other," says Campbell. "Eventually, I chose to graduate them towards the center, as this is the best way to explain the basic construction of the chair. The small-scale paper model contained everything that I was trying to express with the chair: an evident physical strength despite the delicate expression, which was partly thanks to the white paper and partly thanks to the careful cutting. The shadow effects, which are essential to me, worked as intended. And the little model rocked quietly from side to side." Zanotta bought the idea on the basis of the model and never asked any questions about the proposed material or production technique. Louise Campbell returned to Denmark with the assignment of converting the small paper model to a 3D rendering. The two layers of circles, which are identical but scaled in relation to each other, and which give the Very Round Chair its depth effect and strength, needed further work. "My associate Thomas

Louise Campbell (born 1970) has her studio in Copenhagen, serving clients such as Stelton, Muuto and Louis Poulsen. The "Very Round Chair" was made for Zanotta.

The "Very Round Chair" consists of 260 circular shapes, staggered concentrically, scaled and arranged on two levels. The structure is cut by laser from 2mm sheet steel.

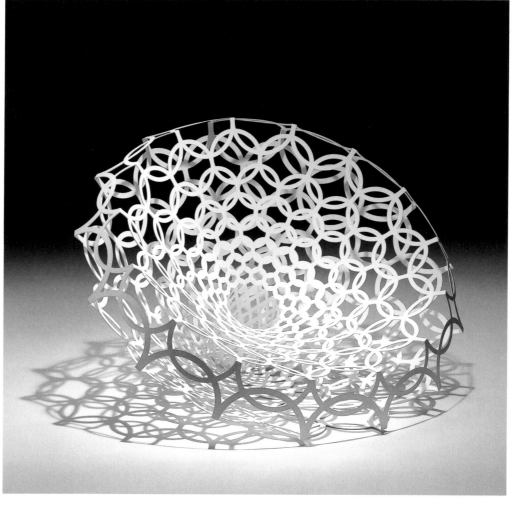

_Zanotta

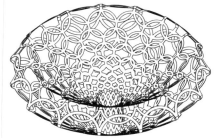

Louise Campbell produced countless models until she arrived at an absolutely perfect shape. The later structure is imprinted on the paper models above.

At the Zanotta furniture factory in Italy, Head of Development Daniele Greppi tests the prototypes (right). The cylinder (above) links they shells and delivers stability.

Bentzen took on the task, which took him over a month to complete, but when the drawing was finished, every last detail was in place, and we were ready for industrial production." From this point, Zanotta took over. "In Denmark we are used to very close collaboration in connection with product development," says the designer. "This process was different. We sat on our hands, waiting to see the result – communicating exclusively via an interpreter, since the head of product development, Daniele Greppi, speaks no English, and I don't speak Italian. Suddenly, we had a photo of the man himself sitting in a perfect prototype, in our in-tray. They showed the same care towards the design that we had." Campbell is convinced that the best designs arise when there are no guidelines: "To convince a highly acknowledged design firm like Zanotta to launch a legless chair that rocks from side to side, and which dares to place aesthetics over comfort, feels like a personal victory." Now, Louise Campbell is able to lean back.

_____ www.louisecampbell.com
_____ www.zanotta.it
_____ Text: Henrik Most

Using refined paper models, Louise Campbell tried out possible structures for the seat weave – and simply using one such model she also convinced Zanotta to build the chair.

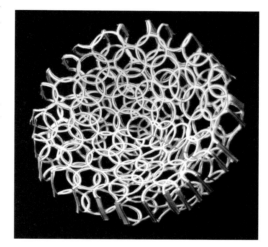

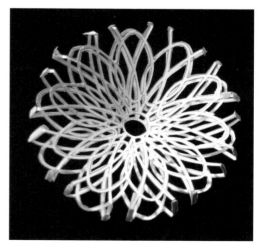

Sturdy and Stackable

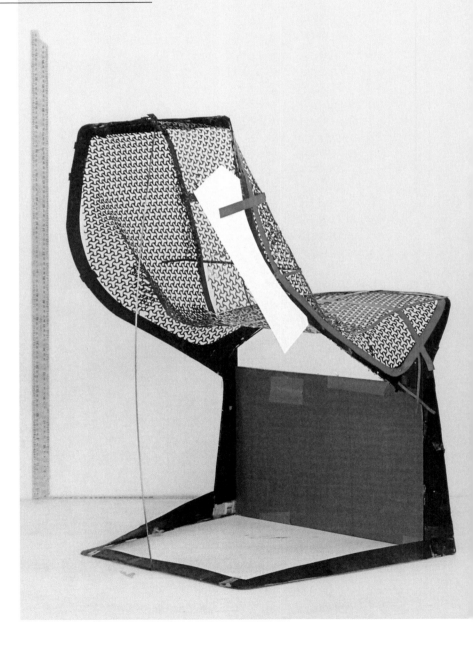

Ever since Verner Panton, no other designer has dared to make a cantilever chair out of plastic – unti now, that is: a completely new material has finally made it possible, namely, Ultradur. For Plank, Konstantin Grcic has formed a swaying chair from the BASF plastic, enriched with nanoparticles, which could very well go down in design history.

_____ One form, one material, one mold. The Myto chair is built as a single unit: its stable frame merges into a net-like backrest and seat which then merges with the body. No wonder that when the eyes first perceive the chair, they glide over prominent edges, soft supports, and trace the transitions. Actually, says Konstantin Grcic, the design came about from a slight misunderstanding, from the false impression that the material can be both soft and hard at the same time. Although the chemists at BASF immediately cleared up this misunderstanding, the desire remained to embrace these opposites as productive tension. The backrest, stretched out like a cushion, arches toward the body. The frame forms an elastic backbone. Myto stays in motion. Polybutylene terephthalate (PBT) is the name of the material which is used first and foremost in the automobile industry, and which BASF markets as Ultradur High Speed. The chemicals giant on the Rhine has developed a particularly fluid technical plastic with it, to which nanoparticles lend special properties. It combines firmness and high fluidity in processing and gives designers completely new possibilities of choosing the cross-sections of their objects freely and of combining thick and thin cross-sections in soft lines. The highly fluid material can be used to create free formal transitions in injection molding, at the same time saving mass.

_____ How did the design come about? In the beginning there was a BASF workshop. Four designers, June 2006 in Ludwigshafen. The chemicals giant wanted something real, ideas about how their own technical plastics, the various Ultras, can vividly demonstrate their strengths. Instead of only highlighting properties like firmness and heat-moldability in the technical documentation, products should be convincing. Afterwards, BASF initially came forward as the only client. The goal was to pave the way for the material's success outside the auto world. Not only as a prototype, but also in mass-produced items. The choice of object and industrial partner was for Grcic to make, which meant: "If it's going to be anything, then it's going to be a chair." And if a chair, then in its most ambitious form, the cantilever. And made of plastic! After takimg this decision, Grcic immediately sensed "liberation, indeed close to lightheadedness," or so he recalls. He had taken on a challenge that all his colleagues had failed

Myto as model: While the red adhesive measuring points can still be seen on the metal mesh of the original model, the intention with the 1:6 models (below) is to select the colors for the end product.

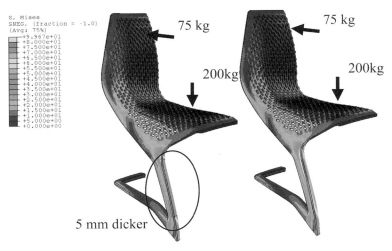

S, Mises
SNEG, (fraction = -1.0)
(Avg: 75%)

+9.967e+01
+8.000e+01
+7.500e+01
+7.000e+01
+6.500e+01
+6.000e+01
+5.500e+01
+5.000e+01
+4.500e+01
+4.000e+01
+3.500e+01
+3.000e+01
+2.500e+01
+2.000e+01
+1.500e+01
+1.000e+01
+5.000e+00
+0.000e+00

75 kg

200kg

5 mm dicker

75 kg

200kg

Konstantin Grcic (right page) and his assistant Alexander Löhr (above) made various versions of the chair using metal mesh up to a genuine size model. The computer-generated frame model (left) reveals potential weak points in the construction when there is a vertical load of 200 kilograms on the chair and there is high backwards load on the backrest.

to address throughout the decades. In order to counter the mixture of complexity, intensity and time pressures, he included the materials manufacturer, the producer, the toolmaker and the machine builders on the team. In the form of Italian company Plank, who had already produced his Miura bar stool for him, and BASF, he had two partners who clearly were willing to learn from each other. And together they pressed the pedal to the metal. Three days before Christmas the first model was complete, and less than two months later Grcic and his assistant Alexander Löhr presented the design to the team, where it was greeted with astonishment and euphoria. The material progressed from cardboard and wire mesh to polystyrene. You could admittedly sit on the milled block, but the model was still supported by a solid core. This was not yet a cantilever by any means. The later mesh for the backrest was simulated by layers of black insulating cable. The chair was covered in patterns. Overly ornamental? Overly dramatic? The design remained in flux, and was then digitized. Engineers at BASF showed on-screen where material needed to be strengthened and where even a thinner wall was possible. In May 2007, Myto progressed from PC to rapid-prototyping model, and the sintered chair took on form. The maker of the final tooling was now also on board. Swiftness and team spirit moved the design process along, eliminating several barriers at once. It celebrated a new and intense coming together of manufacturer, designer and materials

First presentation of the Myto in the studio in Munich: Less than 16 months passed from the BASF workshop to the first public presentation of the prototype at the K-Messe in Düsseldorf.

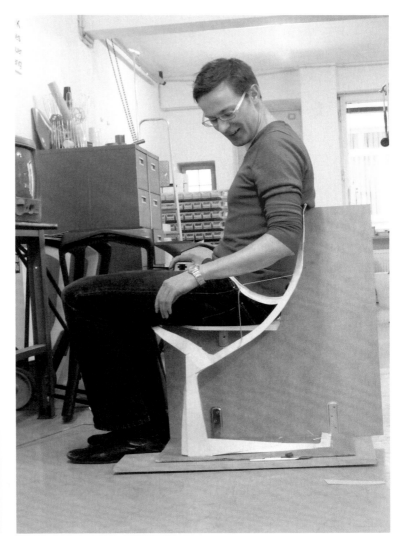

Using a Styrofoam model, Grcic's colleagues simulate various lattice structures with adhesive strips: here a pattern made of overlapping curving strips. Later Grcic opted for a pattern with perforations like those on air vents in trains, for example. Top left: The Munich-based designer talks to Martin Plank from the Italian manufacturer Plank about one of the first models made of wire and card.

Konstantin Grcic working on the prototype (above): Where the rendering below still shows the flowing forms of the original lattice structure, the prototype already displays the final perforated pattern and a yellow-green coating. Myto was ultimately launched in eight colors: bright red, pure orange, light blue, aubergine, yellowish green, black, gray and white gray.

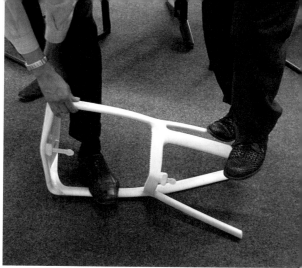

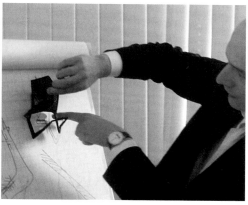

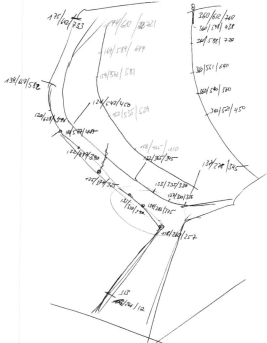

The chair is designed to be stable and yet elastic – hitherto impossible for a plastic cantilever chair. To test the strength of the new BASF material Ultradur High Speed, Plank uses the injection-molded model of Grcic's bar stool Miura, which is generally made using fiberglass-reinforced polypropylene (top). During the first load test on the rapid prototyping Myto model, a wastepaper basket had to be pushed under it (top left); later the chair held on its own. Lorenzo Consolaro of Vivi shows on a 1:6 model how the chair sits in the tool.

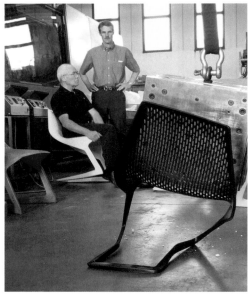

To create lightness, you
need heavy machinery.
Konstantin Grcic lies on the
steel cast. Final load tests
(above) show that the chair
can even withstand a
500-kilogram steel block.

producer, each of them providing their differing areas of expertise. Much was achieved in parallel, and Grcic speaks of the "fruitful flow of information and experience". When Günter Grass philosophized about progress, which he felt moved at a snail's pace, he had society and history in mind, not design. Yet even in the self-proclaimed home country of innovation, most things move far too slowly. Sometimes, however, veritable explosions are to be witnessed. Function follows innovation owing to the nature of the material. "I hope that other companies are encouraged to opt for similar partnerships to handle more complex projects," says Grcic. He has gained a unique experience with plastic: while he previously responded to problems regarding the materials by altering the structures, now it was the material itself that got altered. Suddenly there was a chemist who expanded the material's properties by adding something. "Now these are scientists," Grcic says, "who can turn wishes into a formula." A material that ideally goes through thick and thin. Does he now want to do other things with polybutylene terephthalate? "My mind is still in the last project," he confesses, "my first contact with the material, meaning I am probably inwardly not ready to repeat the risk and adventure. Ultradur and cantilever were the perfect combination." Sounds like the chemistry was right.

_____ www.konstantin-grcic.com
_____ www.basf.de/ultradur
_____ www.plank.it
_____ Text: Oliver Herwig

Under Pressure

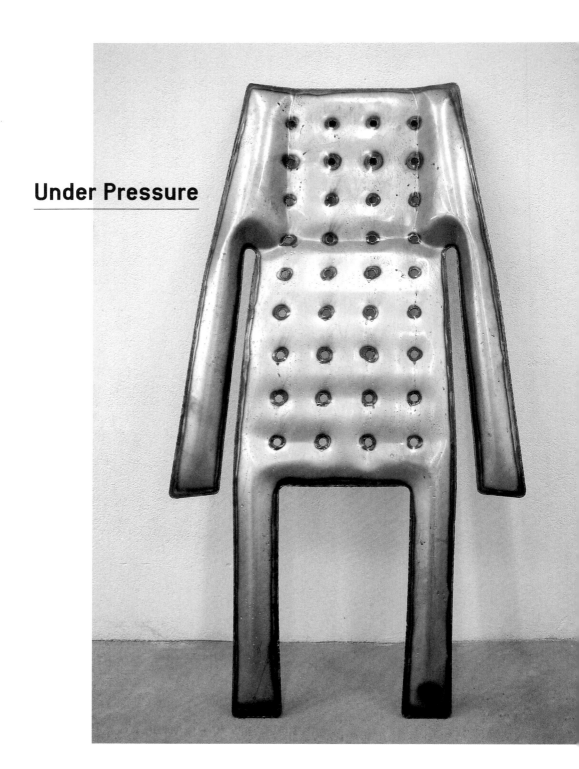

Designers, architects and engineers have always tried to make sheet metal stable. Corrugated iron is one option but the thin, elastic and inexpensive material can also be made robust through bending or bulging it. Polish architect Oskar Zieta even creates inflatable furniture and entire bridges. Just how does that work?

_____ Oskar Zieta's first item of furniture might bear a vague resemblance to those inflatable rubber animals that children take into swimming pools in the summer. The stool looks as light as a feather and highly elastic. However, in reality it weighs in at 3.1 kilos. And it does not budge one millimeter. Yet it really is inflated; this is not an optical illusion. That said, what has been blown up is not a plastic but 0.8 mm-thin sheet steel. "The stool is a kind of manifesto of our technology," says Zieta solemnly. For three years the young Pole and his colleague Philipp Dohmen at the ETH Zurich have worked on a production technology that they call "free internal pressure deformation" (FiDU). It is a method that can best be compared with hydroforming used in the automobile industry. However, the technology developed by the two architects is by no means as complex and manages with one thousandth of the pressure.

It looks filigree, but is stable: the inflated sheet-metal shape can bear up to five people (above). The first inflated model, not yet bent to form a chair, looks like a sculpture (left).

_____ "What makes this so special is how quickly and accurately rigid elements can be produced; in other words, a three-dimensional object can be made from a two-dimensional sheet," says Zieta. Using a flatbed laser cutting machine, two identically shaped sheets are cut, placed on top of each other and then welded together at the edges. Subsequently, the space between the sheets can be expanded using air pressure (0.1 to 7 bar) until the desired shape is achieved. Initially, Zieta and Dohmen experimented with water pressure but meanwhile they have opted for air pressure and applied for a patent for the FiDU technology. As Philipp Dohmen explains the inflation of the steel is not the decisive factor – he compares this to stacking boxes – which is to be patented, but rather the calculations the two use to control the process of inflation – specifically, the parameters including things such as form and thickness of the steel sheeting, internal pressure and deformation time.

_____ Zieta, born 1975, is convinced that the FiDU technology is not only suitable for furniture design, but can also be applied for larger-scale objects, mechanical engineering and architectural applications: "This is a flexible technology with a wide range of application areas." Anyhow, it is early days yet. Things get complicated if you wish to calculate in advance what you need to do so that the metal deforms as desired. Zieta uses digital chains by which the process between design, construction and production is not

Zieta and Dohmen initially experimented with pressurized water. However, compressed air is better suited to pump up the welded sheet-metal sections. The process has since been registered for a patent.

interrupted and data from a wide variety of sources are combined. For example, if the stool did not have a hole in the middle of the seating area, the latter would inflate to form an enormous cushion, and the legs would remain flat. This is why for Zieta's second furniture design – the Plopp chair – the designer is planning a regular perforated pattern on the seat and backrest. Although this requires accurate workmanship, it does ensure that the sheet steel is only slightly deformed, making for a comfortable seat. Originally it was to be called Chippensteel because the perforations were reminiscent of the button padding characteristically found in Chippendale furniture. It took a great deal of experimentation before Zieta and Dohmen realized you have to taper the cross-section of the steel at the points you wish to bend it. Gaining acceptance for a new technology is anything but easy. Zieta now knows that by his own experience. "For two years we have been trying to get the FIDU technology promoted", he says. And you could say the stool acts as his demonstration model. He has presented it at various fairs including the one in Milan and the Munich Designparcours, and he has contacted potential manufacturers. But nobody wanted to produce the stool – even though it looks so simple and self-explanatory. So Zieta decided to build his own plant: it is located in Zielona Góra, Poland, not far from the German border. Then, as luck would have it, the ETH Zurich was keen to sell the broken laser cutting machine that Zieta had already worked with for years. It took two trucks to transport the laser, and six months before it worked again properly. Zieta got himself a welding robot, made a second semi-automatic robot, and is now preparing the serial production of the stool having already secured Danish furniture firm Hay as distribution partner. "It might be fun but it is also incredibly complicated," says Zieta. The chair is to follow, and designs for a bench and a table also exist.

_____ In future, even more complex shapes will be possible using the FIDU technology. Last winter, Zieta and his students built a 6-meter-long steel bridge that weighs 174 kilos yet withstood a test load of just under two tons easily. Prior to cutting, they rolled up the 1 mm-thick steel sheeting, transported it by bus, and then inflated it at the ETH using a conventional air compressor. "In fact, you could easily have used a bicycle pump," says Zieta – only 0.4 bar air pressure was necessary. He and his students have also produced steel replicas of classic chairs by Ron Arad, Jasper Morisson, Charles Eames and Max Bill through to Gerrit Rietveld – which were then blown up to caricatures of themselves. Honi soit …

_____ www.zieta.pl
_____ www.blech.arch.ethz.ch
_____ www.hay.dk
_____ Text: Jenny Keller

Oskar Zieta (born 1975) is actually an architect. However, he has been very successful with his first item of furniture: The stool version of the inflatable item is called "Plopp", and is now sold by Danish company Hay – and has, among other things, won the red dot award.

When welding the two sheets of metal together a stencil makes certain that the parts do not shift out of line. A valve is positioned on the laser-welded contour line (below). Zieta's inflatable furniture items exploit the full potential of CNC manufacturing and FIDU molding (Free-Inner-Pressure Molding). The result: a chair that seems feather-light but is extremely stable (right).

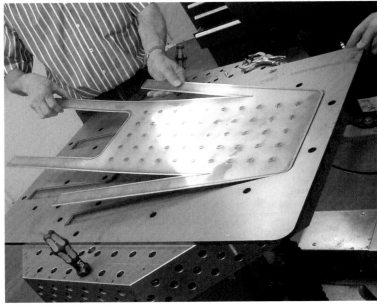

Interiors

Once Upon a Wall

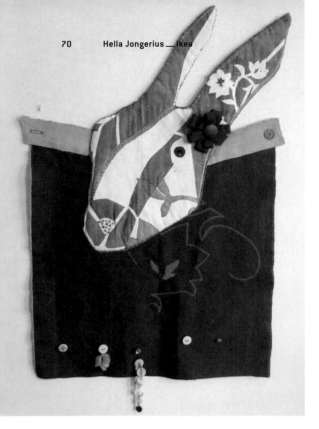

The semi-industrial production of the tapestries is elaborate: The printed motif of the animal head is quilted onto the respective backing textile in red or black to create a 3D effect (above l.). Countless studies were necessary to get to the final design for the tapestries (on the r.). Among other things, old Swedish textiles were taken as the model here (upper r.)

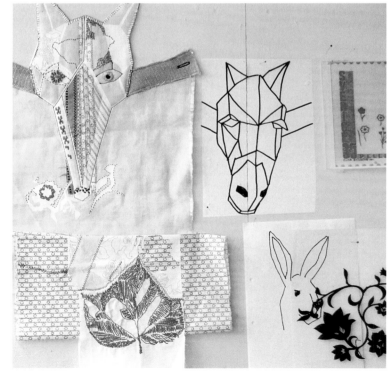

In Hella Jongerius' new project for Ikea, she has come up with decorative designs: her animal motif wall hangings are part of the 2009 PS Collection, for which Ikea also commissioned well-known designers such as Front. The hangings are quilted, embroidered and even signed in India.

_____ When 50 products of the new PS collection appeared on the shelves of European Ikea stores, design collectors had to hurry in order to get hold of one of Hella Jongerius' products. That is because Gullspira, Mikkel and Pelle, the three wool and cotton-quilted, 70 by 93 centimeter hangings boasting goat, fox, and hare motifs, will initially only be produced in a first run of 10,000. For Ikea this is a diminutive number. By way of comparison, for the launch of the PS collection in 2006, 100,000 of the Jonsberg vase series, Hella Jongerius' first design for the company, were produced. "The new wall decorations represent a kind of arty edition within our product range," says Peter Klinkert, project manager of the current PS edition.

_____ In this case, from the outset the product development was geared less to a top-selling mass product and more to integrate sustainability in the production process as well as, in co-operation with Unicef, continuing to build up a location established in India. "For us, the PS collection was always a starting point from which to discover new things, be it new materials or production methods," Klinkert says. "We see the manufacture of textiles as a step towards implementing workshops and know-how in the Uttar Pradesh region. Hella's product demonstrates how we could provide sustainable results on a long-term basis." The work in the textile workshop currently provides financial security for some 1,800 women from a total of 500 villages, enabling them to send their children to school, thereby helping to prevent child labor. This social aspect was crucial for Jongerius' decision to work for Ikea again. "I found the prospect of working for a non-profit-niche of this major cooperation exciting," she says.

_____ The working title of the new PS collection is "Roots of Sweden" for which, in addition to Hella Jongerius, a number of in-house designers and, for the first time, the Swedish group Front were commissioned. The products were to be made of traditional materials such as solid wood and wool, to justify the claim to sustainability and durability, or to reference role models in Swedish history. From the first meeting in the development center in Älmhult, Jongerius, together with the PS design team, went to Skansen, a museum village near Stockholm, where alongside traditional constructions, historical furniture and home textiles are also on view. Looking back she says: "It was only here that the brief took specific form. My concrete assignment was ultimately to design a textile wall decoration that referred to Swedish roots and was to be made in India."

_____ So as not to drift into the folklore scene – "the idea of 1970s fake art hippy wall hangings horrified me", – Jongerius used three typical animal

Hella Jongerius traveled twice to India herself where together with a staff member she showed the women the right way to make the tapestries.

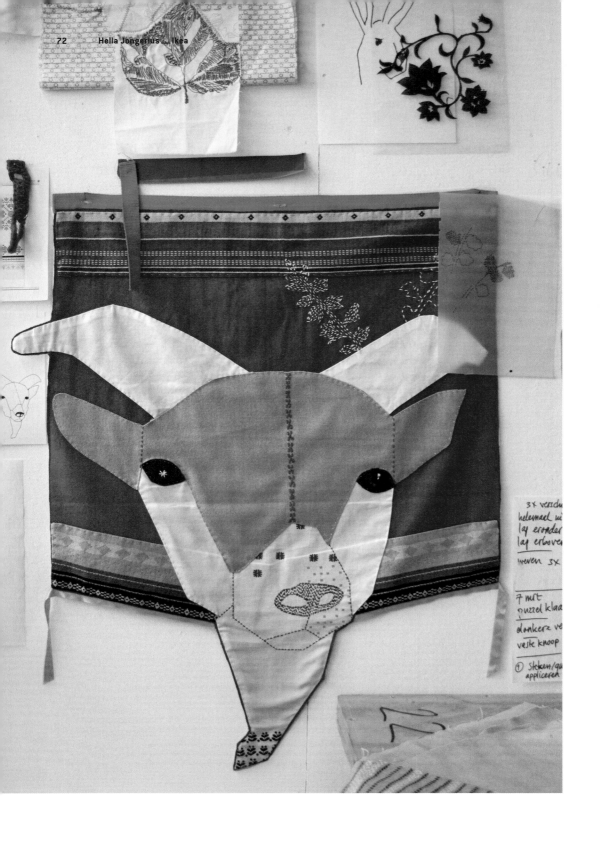

For her collection Jongerius
created abstract heads of
the animals that occur most
frequently in Swedish fairy-
tales – hare, goat (left)
and fox. To be able to make
the tapestries, the women
in Uttar Pradesh had to
learn ten different embroidery stitches.
Below: Jongerius herself
works on embroidering.

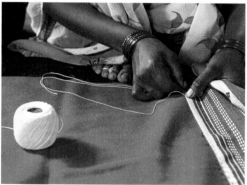

Hella Jongerius feels the social side to the project is the very important. The Unicef workshop enabled the women to become financially independent and send their children to school.

motifs from classic Swedish tales. "Animals appear continually in my works, for instance in the Animal Bowls for Nymphenburg or in the Office Pets for Kreo. This kind of figurative display appeals to children and adults and gave us an opportunity to give the hangings spatial depth." Jongerius' first step was to design abstract heads of a hare, a fox and a goat as three-dimensional masks, which she then transferred to a quilt of various layers of monochrome or printed fabrics, embroidery and appliqué, borders and passament. Jongerius designed every detail from the six different foundation textiles to the borders herself – even if the patterns and ornaments are based on history. With three prototypes ready for production in her suitcase, in 2007 she traveled to India for the first time, where together with a colleague, the fabric designer Edith van Berkel and an Ikea team, she taught the first group of unskilled workers the art of quilting and ten different embroidering techniques. "Using a pre-fabricated kit, each seamstress had to learn how to produce a complete wall decoration from beginning to end and, in addition, how to train further seamstresses," says the renowned Dutch designer. "We soon found out which bits were too complex or took up too much time." She subsequently modified three designs before making her final decision.

_____ The three wall hangings are a typical Hella Jongerius product: they are made of industrially made yarn but finished purely by hand. The fusion of traditional craftsmanship with industrial processes and giving mass-produced products an individual touch has long since become one of Jongerius' trademarks. In the case of the Jonsberg vases, which were produced in Chinese ceramic factories, this was shown by the hand-made perforated patterns which, though they followed the designer's instructions, ultimately bore the signature of the individual worker, making each vase unique. The wall hangings, on the other hand, are quilted and embroidered by hand, each one taking a day and a half – the individualization process ending with each article being signed: the seamstress herself embroiders her initials in Hindi.

_____ www.jongeriuslab.com
_____ www.ikea.com
_____ Text: Kristina Raderschad

Where Mikkel the fox, Pelle the hare and Gullspira the goat say good night: These are the final designs for the Ikea PS Collection. They were initially made in an edition of 10,000 — a relatively low number for Ikea: the wall hangings are rated more as an art edition.

The Power of Patterns

The Spanish designer Patricia Urquiola is considered one of the world's most renowned, and also most productive, female designers. Now, for the first time, she has designed a porcelain service for Rosenthal. It is the story of a balancing act between creative ambition and the technically feasible.

_____ Patricia Urquiola is known for not being scared to use classic arts and crafts techniques such as sewing, knitting and crocheting. Indeed, the Spanish designer, who works in Milan, uses these techniques to create any number of unique, multi-layered surface moldings, which are as delightful to touch as they are a feast for the eyes. And as a rule she links these details closely with the construction, such that they go beyond pure decoration. Her designs cannot be catego-rized conventionally at all – they place comfort above purely scientific ergonomics and a sensory quality above the sometimes unexpressive aes-thetics of functionalism. Hardly surprising, then, that she has also produced extraordinary results when working with porcelain for the first time. The dinner service Landscape, which along with porcelain includes glassware, cutlery and table linen, brings a new disorder to the table: differ-ent relief modings, of which there are seven in total, cover the rimless plates, cups and bowls. They do not stop either at the edge of the plates or the bottom of the cups and continue on to the cutlery and table linen. Plain symmetry and the central arrangement of decor are things of the past.

Patricia Urquiola worked in porcelain for the first time for Rosenthal. Left: Cup with a paper model of the handle.

_____ "When Rosenthal asked me if I wanted to design a dinner service, I was instantly sure of one thing: the traditional porcelain service with its pre-cise number of pieces is obsolete", says Urquiola. "It was important to me that each piece have a different relief and all the pieces are individual enough to be attractive in their own right. However, a porcelain dinner serv-ice with such a complex design should appeal to a broad public, not just wedding list customers." Her motto: combine as the mood takes you. As such there are, for example, under plates, breakfast plates, dinner plates and soup bowls and the matching serving dishes down to the sauce boat – concessions to the classic order of the menu. Yet the different relief struc-tures do not allow an all too rigid place setting in the first place. And, on top of that, there is a large selection of bowls in various sizes, starting with a diameter of seven centimeters, which caters to new eating habits. The small

Seven different reliefs spread across the surface of the china like a virus in the Landscape series, growing over the edges. The reliefs are designed in negative molds (right), and the porcelain bowls are then press-molded isostatically.

bowls are suitable for finger food and snacks, as well as for meals which are served in no particular hierarchical order, for example, Spanish tapas and oriental mezze. Urquiola invites us to take a spontaneous and very playful approach to her service.

⎯⎯⎯⎯ Even though it was certainly not easy, Patricia Urquiola succeeded in transferring her partiality to multi-layered reliefs to porcelain. She worked with the material, manipulating it as easily as if it were fabric. Parts of the reliefs cover the plates and bowls like a fine veil, others like embroidery. In other places they sit on the porcelain like crochet edging, or serve as handles or grips. In order to realize the relief detailing all of which have differing depths, especially the curved shapes, the development department at Rosenthal had to make use of all the tricks of the trade. "The challenge was to transfer the digitized drawings from the Urquiola studio into three-dimensional shapes", says Head of Development Robert Suk. However, he declines to reveal exactly how they did this, given the competition. "But the fact that we were using bespoke porcelain is important to gain an understanding." Mister Suk can say this much: "To generate 3D structures from the 2D graphics, we developed a special technique in the model construction phase which enabled us to produce the relief structure in rapid prototyping, then place it in the curved plaster mold and thus create the basic shape step by step."

Urquiola chose the best positioning for the patterns on the bowls and plates using printed paper models.

The digital drawings show the patterns that arise from superimposed reliefs. Initially made as flat paper shapes (right), they are later transposed into 3D forms (bottom left).

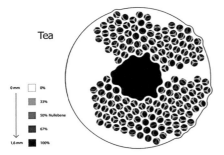

Tea

0 mm
0%
33%
50% Nullebene
67%
1,6 mm
100%

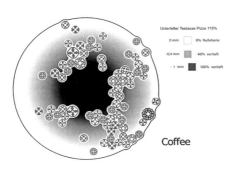

Unterteller Teetasse Pizzo 115%

0 mm   0% Nullebene
-0,4 mm   40% vertieft
- 1 mm   100% vertieft

Coffee

Espresso

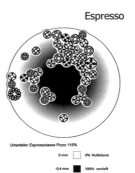

Unterteller Espressotasse Pizzo 115%

0 mm   0% Nullebene
-0,4 mm   100% vertieft

"We have transferred the quality of a hand-crafted product into a mass-made item," Urquiola says (in conversation with Robert Suk, Head of Product Development at Rosenthal). Above you can see the negative molds for the china. Urquiola covered not only the tableware with these meandering motifs, but also the cutlery (see above).

_____ Compared with the model and tool construction, the manufacture of the service did not require any fundamental innovations: The plates were isostatically pressed, the cups were thrown and hollow pieces, i.e., vases and jugs, were cast. Another special feature of Landscape, also compared with other Studio Line services by Rosenthal, is the extremely thin porcelain. The thickness of the cup, for example, is just 1.2 millimeters, which requires great care during the throwing process – a further challenge for the German porcelain manufacturer, fully in tune with Urquiola: "I wanted to test the limits of this traditional company, using its own means. I wanted to make the thinnest china industrial production allows." Thus in the light, the individual pieces seem transparent, which is extremely unusual with hard porcelain, unlike bone china. Urquiola compares the reliefs to "viruses which penetrate the porcelain and hollow it out from the inside". When looking at the pieces against the light, the structure of the seven reliefs (Circles, Grid, Dots, Leaves, Folk, Electro and Pizzo) becomes visible in up to three levels. Pizzo and Folk are comparatively simple in terms of construction, although the motifs already bear Urquiola's signature: Pizzo calls to mind lace, and Folk woven textures. Her design approach comes into full bloom in the reliefs Circles and Grid, each structured into three levels. Suk explains the genesis of the three levels, using Circles as an example: "If you place three perforated metal sheets on top of each other and then turn them to face each other, they create a new picture. In this case they almost resemble flowers." A similar process forms the basis of the honeycomb-shaped Grid, only here a finely woven grid served as the template. Patricia Urquiola transferred the interrupted structures of perforated metal sheets and grids to porcelain and alienated them in such a way as to create decorative motifs. In this way, she once again demonstrated her skill in adopting constructive templates and making sensory surfaces from them. Landscape may be her first exploration of porcelain, but the service effortlessly slots into place on the long list of her designs which surprise in both tactile and visual terms. We will probably be seeing more of this.

_____ www.patriciaurquiola.com
_____ www.rosenthal.de
_____ Text: Karianne Fogelberg

The different structures generate different degrees of transparency – their beauty comes into its own when they are held up against the light (below).

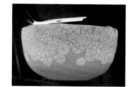

A Bag of Tricks

No doubt about it: Munich-based designer Stefan Diez has reinvented the shoulder bag. Neither clips nor seams interfere with the clean external appearance of the new product range of Authentics. This is achieved using sealed edges.

———— Snow has started to melt around the mud, gravel and puddles. If you go to visit Stefan Diez you have to climb behind houses in Munich's Glockenbach district, wade through sludge and squeeze past wooden sheds. His workshop is out on the water, with a narrow staircase leading up to the top as if one were ascending to the bridge of a ship. There, computers hum while plywood slats creak underfoot. Everything has been patched together and stands witness to ingenious improvisation. It is that mix of simplicity and finesse that characterizes many of his works, such as the Kuvert range of bags for Authentics, with which Diez began to experiment two years ago. He wanted to create something "of low complexity", without conspicuous fastenings and inside seams, a combination of synthetics and textiles, elegant, simple and consistent. Something that has what it takes to go down as a classic and can be expanded into a whole range of bags, from utility and casual bags, covering the spectrum from necessaires, shoulder bags and city bags.

———— The first paper models look like American shopping bags that have fallen into the hands of a Japanese designer, been reduced to the essentials and then sculpted. They have an inside-out Y-seam giving stability and an edging into which expanded metal is later placed, to seal the whole thing and make it light as a feather. Such a clear form. And yet complex problems came along with it, namely, open edges and missing fastenings. Bags have a natural weak spot, that is, their seams. To protect this Achilles heel, they are either sewn on the inside and then turned the right way round, which can easily lead to complicated geometrical problems, or a second layer of material, which lies around the edges like a U that has been rolled inward, has to protect the seams. Aesthetically highly displeasing, according to Diez. Why not just cut straight edges, instead of sewing them together in a complicated way? Diez coated fabric with a liquid synthetic material and ironed it on, creating a type of truck tarpaulin, but coated only on one side. The synthetic emulsion heat-bonds with the base layer, made from material, linen or fabric, forming a high-tech textile that can be cut in a straight line at any place. An ideal material to start with. Edges can be ironed, zips stuck on fast, even star-shaped inset cuts, as used in some of the smaller models to substantially increase volume, are no problem. And yet, the irritating problem of the

A clear matter: The shoulder bag Kuvert as pre-production model. It is made of polyester coated with PVC. Initially Stefan Diez simulated the effect with simple adhesive foil (left page).

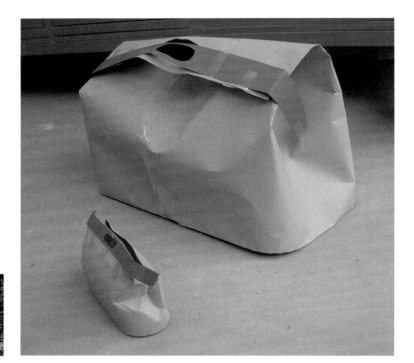

Stefan Diez sealed the very first models with gray rubber flaps. He worked with paper for a long time before making the prototypes of the various bags (below).

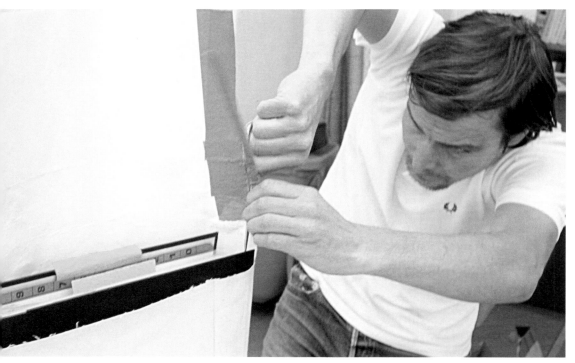

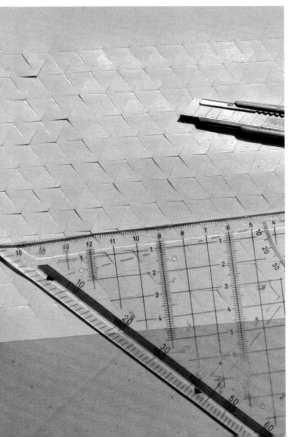

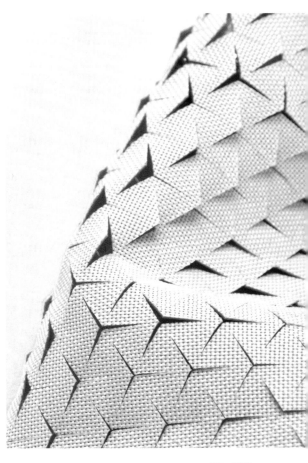

The type of meshes used in metal construction served as the template for the star pattern, which is as decorative as it is functional – making the bag elastic and permeable to air. Special software helped draw the pattern (top left). The two notches mark the places where the shoulder strap will later be attached. Right: Stefan Diez talking to the owners of Authentics, Elmar (right) and Hendrik Flötotto.

First experiments: Hannes Gumpp, an assistent to Diez, used a stencil to apply a dot grid made of rubber – the rubber surfaces were used so that holes could be stamped without cutting them. Later on the designers preferred to coat entire fabric backs.

After dyeing, Christian Jagdhuber washes down the previously coated material using a garden hose. A PVC emulsion often used in T-shirt printing serves as the coating material. In the workshop Hannes Gumpp still works with an iron (left); in the Chinese factory the edges are high-frequency sealed.

edges fraying with every cut was only solved at the very end of the project: Hendrik Flötotto suggested a new base material, namely, polyester instead of cotton. The secret of clean edges is singeing, says Diez, holding his lighter up to the bag and grinning. "Why should I not take advantage of the experiences others have made?"

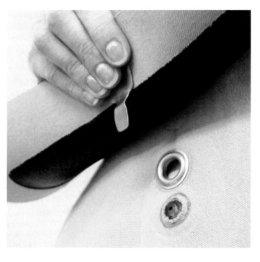

_____ It goes without saying, every stud fastener, every rivet would have destroyed the bag's quiet, natural form. Thus all fasteners added on to the various bags had to go. As an alternative, Diez also experimented with welded-on rubber fasteners that hang from the bags like ripcords. "There are a hell of a lot of solutions on the market already," as he had to admit when he started on the research and drew up what amounted to a typology of fastenings, including all the buttons, studs and straps. Anything went, as long as they were not visible. So his team endeavored to pack all the technical elements inside the bag, right down to the shoulder strap adjustments. Up the creek in the name of aesthetics. Finally, three basic models won out: specifically, zips that grow together directly with the material, welded-on rubber fasteners with ring anchors and invisible hook fasteners on the inside of the bags. You insert the metal clip into a ring, flip it down over the ring, and then it holds in place. Diez does not wax philosophical about his range of bags, neither is he secretive about his methods: "It is always difficult at the beginning", the 35-year-old suggests, who also recalls that he hesitated for a long time before completing the first step. After that it became easier. Only when everything is going smoothly and the first solutions have been developed does Diez increase the complexity of his design process. Then he adds colors, oil paints from a painting store, or adopts completely new production processes using a heating press from a carpentry workshop. The main policy: it has to be possible to go ahaed and experiment with it. "Nothing is too difficult for us, or too strenuous", he claims. For him, design is like a pasta sauce you toy around with for a long time. "Sometimes you have to start again". The recipe for Kuvert now stands on firm ground. Nothing else is going to burn on the hob. And if, perhaps, the edges start to fray, simply singe them.

Let's lock it up for good: a bent hook is attached to an eyelet and the bag flap is closed, both being completely invisible.

_____ www.stefandiez.com
_____ www.authentics.de
_____ Text: Oliver Herwig

Once the flap has been hooked in place you can't get a hand in the bag. The trick: a bent edge that arises because the strap is fastened on the sides (right). The cosmetics bag stretches and breathes thanks to the pattern stamped into it (above).

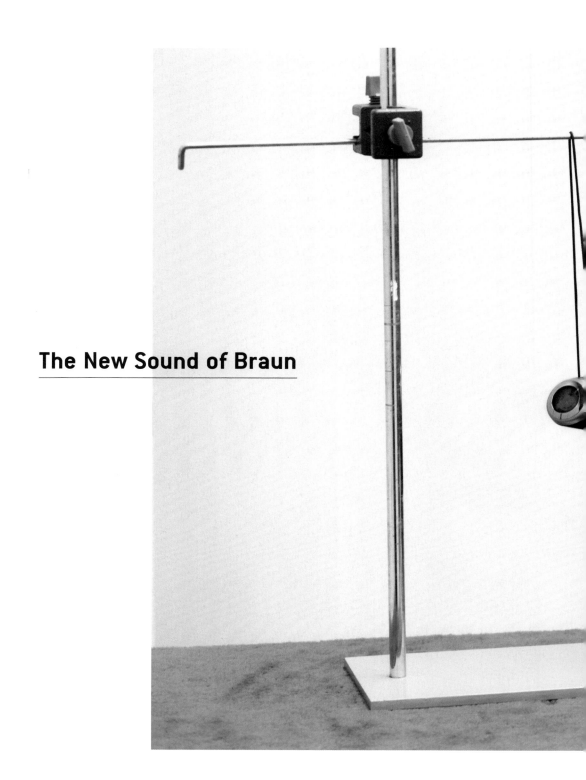

The New Sound of Braun

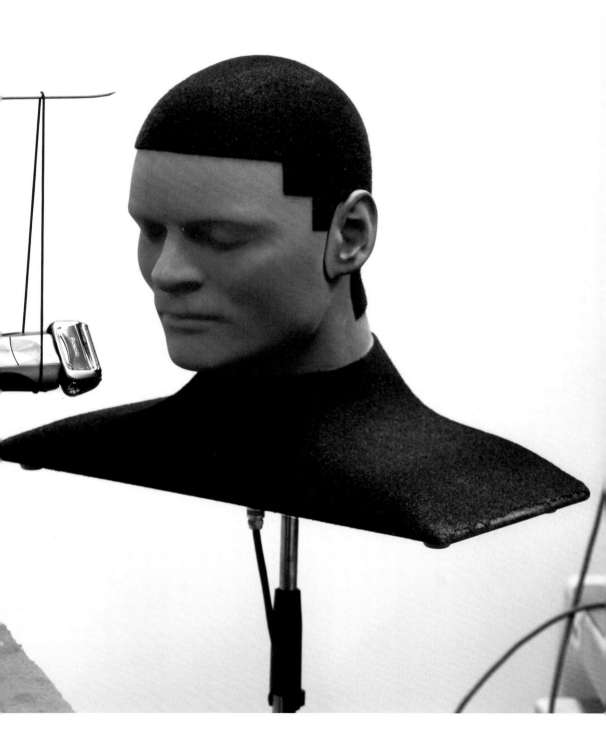

Pulsonic is a new type of razor: a clear distinction between the ergonomically shaped handle as a functional element and the considerably wider shaving head defines the model. "My goal was to design a tool for men", says Braun designer Roland Ullmann. As you can see from the sketches below, the flexible shaving head can be opened on one side by pressing a button, and locked in place on the other side.

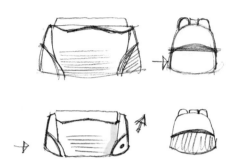

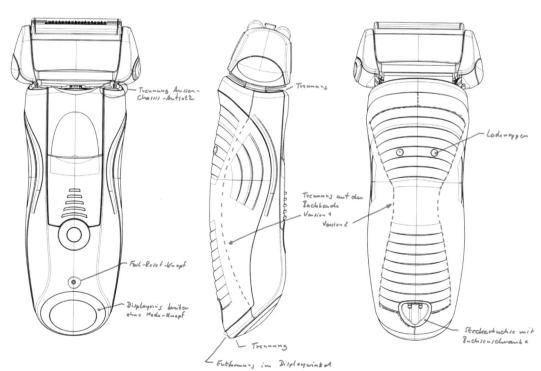

37 years ago Roland Ullmann designed his first shaver for Braun. Since then, he has designed more than one hundred subsequent models; one of the most surprising, however, is the newest: Ullmann has made a real tool of the Pulsonic, whose striking sound is produced by a special sonic motor.

———— Back in 1972, while still a student, it was not really his choice when Dieter Rams guided him to Braun. However, the first task he was given was not to work on the newest hi-fi study but on a shaver. And then the next one. Somehow it just seemed to work out that way; before becoming a stundent at the Offenbach school of design, Roland Ullmann had already completed an apprenticeship as an electrical engineering technician at Siemens. "Making shavers was simply my twist of fate," says Ullmann. He has designed well over 100 models that have gone on the market – no other designer has influenced shaver history quite like he has, not to mention the countless patents. Ullmann fused soft rubber knobs with hard surfaces for the Micron so that the device would be easier to hold: it was the beginning of the hard/soft technology. He made the shaver a lot slimmer by integrating an outer shell structure and a central plug connector in the Vario 3. And he designed the first moveable cutting head, and later, the first to have an internal suspension function. Today, the 60-year-old is still at Braun, the longest-serving of eight industrial designers in Kronberg. What does he make of the radical change, i.e., the fact the company is now part of a global group and is bidding farewell to Braun's legendary objectivity? And what do the products which Ullmann now designs have in common with those from the early days?

———— At first glance, not much, if you look at the recently introduced Pulsonic premium model. And yet much more than Braun critics always claim. Because the new Pulsonic includes all that was important in Ullmann's path-breaking ideas over the last 37 years. On the one hand, the new model is the sum of all of them, yet, on the other, according to Ullmann, "there is nothing in this model which is not new. It is sensational, even for us." What is distinctly new is: the sonic motor, which has the cutting head vibrating at a frequency of up to 180 Hertz – in this way, facial hair, even in problem zones, is supposed to stand upright; and the rotating head which can be

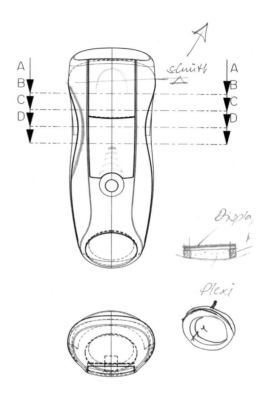

How can you integrate a circular display to show how much battery life is remaining? Which shape is the most ergonomic? This drawing addresses details of the handle.

Senior designer at Braun: Roland Ullmann has been with the company since 1972 and today is responsible for the Male Hair Removal and Advanced Design divisions.

positioned at an angle two times that of the previous model thanks to the spring-loaded cutting blades. Roland Ullmann was decisively involved in this particular development. But he also used the technology to design a very different type of shaver: "My aim was to design a tool for men." Ullmann's first sketches already show the clear separation between the handle and the functional element, i.e. the cutting head which is somewhat wider. He slimmed down the body of the shaver yet again, slightly tapered it and integrated ergonomic depressions for the thumb etc. The hard/soft technology has also been used again: Ullmann used more rubber than ever so that the device fits in your hand just like a battery-powered screwdriver. A closed black surface set off with grooves. The design clearly sets itself apart from its predecessors – those harmoniously proportioned, compact units.

_____ However, it took two years before the new concept caught on. During this time components and systems were tested world-wide. Only then did Ullmann define the outer shape – with a pencil and in the CAD program ProEngineer. It was a shape which then barely changed until the end of the design process. What did constantly change, however, was the design of the surface. The management found the proven pattern of rubber dots (which in the end served more as orientation than as grip) overly nostalgic. And there were also a number of variations in features on the inner side of the Pulsonic: a blue LED dot and wave-like ripples and grooves suggest the power of the sonic motor – something Roland Ullmann would have formerly omitted. "It is pretty clear that here emotional elements have to be added to the 'form follows function' concept. The perfect simplicity which Braun used to be known for doesn't work any more." In tests conducted in many countries it was revealed that "people find it difficult to sell products which lack emotion," according to Ullmann. "We no longer sell just to aesthetes, but to perfectly normal people as well." He had to adapt but understands his great responsibility – after all, the shaver division generates close on half Braun's total sales. "Today we cannot afford for a product development to flop," he comments. This despite the fact that he works on ten or twelve products simultaneously. While Ullmann is busy working on a successor to the successor, the Pulsonic is currently still being improved in the sound lab. The focus is on the noise that occurs when the blades meet beard whiskers: The high speed of the blades has eliminated the sound and quite some efforts are now being made to recreate it.

_____ www.braun.com
_____ Text: Markus Zehentbauer

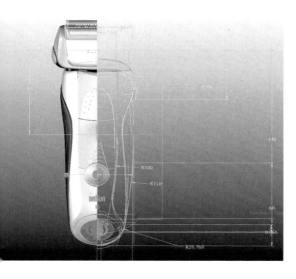

Genesis of a shaver: volume study using acrylic foam, CNC-cut plastic models, a painted version and the end product. Top: various surface textures for the thumb depression on the inside. Left: representation using the CAD program ProEngineer.

Sound designer Wolfgang Brey was responsible for the sound of the Pulsonic. He recorded the whirring sound in a soundproofed room to filter out potential interference factors.

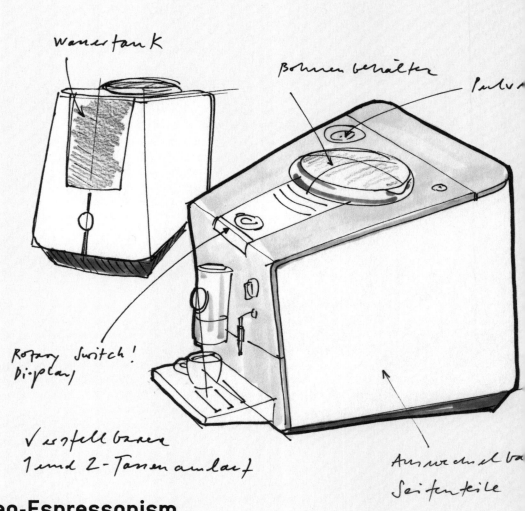

Wassertank

Bohnen behälter

Pulv

Rotary Switch!
Display

Verstellbarer
1 und 2 - Tassenauslauf

Auswechselba
Seitenteile

Neo-Espressonism

Anyone planning to buy a professional espresso machine usually first has to make room in their kitchen. Now, the Swiss manufacturer Jura has launched a very slender, fully automatic coffee machine onto the market: Ena is barely wider than a sheet of paper. Here, we show you how the design became the product.

_____ What could the world's most slender espresso machine look like? For two and a half years the Zurich-based designers Ronald Büttler and Manuel Candio pondered this question. And it was also the basic question in a competition the Swiss company Jura Elektroapparate AG invited several designers to participate in. Candio & Büttler probably came out on top because their design seems even slimmer than it actually is. For the duo created a trapezoidal casing which tapers towards the top and which measures just 21 centimeters at its narrowest point – the same width as a sheet of A4 paper. The industrial designer Ronald Büttler and architect Manuel Candio take on all kinds of design jobs: they design products, rooms and entire buildings. However, as far as coffee machines are concerned, Büttler is an expert. He worked for the former Jura designer, Werner Zemp, for five years. Ena is, therefore, not his first coffee machine design, but the first of which he was in full control. The brief for Ena was for a machine which would be different from the other Jura fully automatic coffee machines while still boasting the typical values of the company. "Ronald Büttler made two excellent proposals, on the basis of which he landed the contract," says Emanuel Probst, General Manager of Jura, who likes to make comparisons with the automobile industry. "Cool Nordic design" is the term he has set his sights on for all Jura products. A coffee machine, according to Probst, should express the same as a Mercedes or an Audi, which both stand for quality and longevity.

Ronald Büttler (left) and Manuel Candio have created the most slender coffee machine in the world. Above, discussing the details using foam models. Opposite: a sketch showing how the water and the coffee beans are meant to remain visible behind transparent covers.

_____ However, in the first instance the design was based on the competition guidelines, in which the configuration of the purely technical, standardized components was already sketched out. On this basis, coming up with extraordinary solutions was no easy task. As such the orthogonal coffee bean container, which, according to the documents, was to be located in one corner of the casing, became circular and was positioned in the center. "A challenge," as Büttler says. Alongside designing a new model, the product developers at Jura are constantly working on new components which are then integrated to coincide with the launch of a new appliance. As regards Ena, this was the case with the zero energy switch, which after

30 minutes cuts the machine's connection to the electricity supply completely, such that there are no stand-by costs. For this reason the German Energy Agency recently dubbed Ena the most energy-efficient, fully automatic coffee machine.

_____ Ronald Büttler's aim was to design a simple machine which is simple to use. He did not use curves or bulges, just straight lines, surfaces and radii. And still there are no right angles. The casing not only tapers towards the top, it also leans forward. A momentum dynamic, balanced by the coffe spout. "For me, this gesture of the machine leaning forward and offering its services is very important. It comes up to you and presents the cups and the coffee." The way in which functional elements like the coffee bean container at the top, the water tank on the back, which both have transparent covers, and the coffee spout are presented is striking. Actually, according to Büttler, it is now customary to cover everything on a coffee machine and hide it behind little doors: "I am pleased that using a very straightforward formal language we have succeeded in making something with individual character." The most difficult thing was controlling the shape, because the on-screen representation of different perspectives always exaggerated the slanted features and trapezoidal shape. Therefore Büttler and the developers at Jura focused on working with models.

Steps en route to choosing the shape: various models from the competition phase (below).

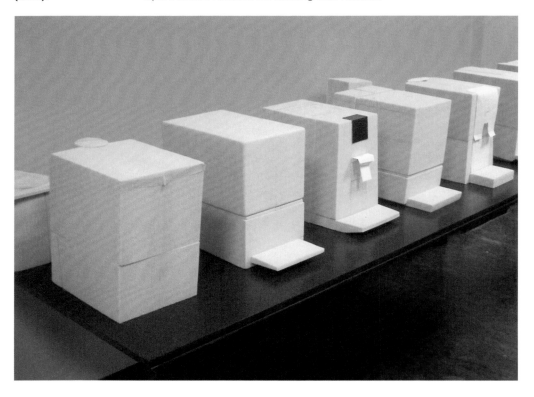

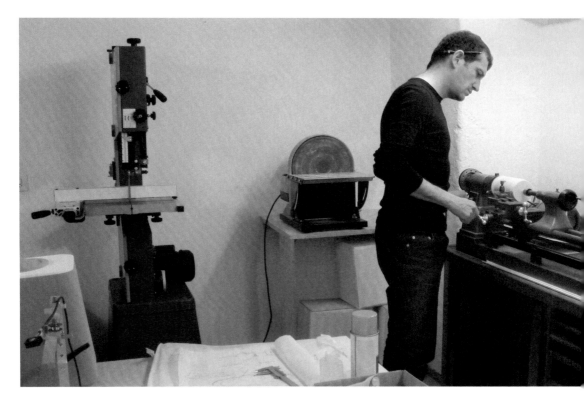

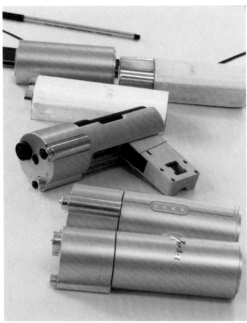

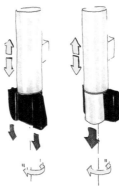

Ronald Büttler working in his Zurich model-building workshop (above). He is a coffee machine specialist: He spent five years working for the former in-house designer at Jura, Werner Zemp. Left: a sketched idea for the coffee spout: by turning the cylinder you can choose one or two cups.

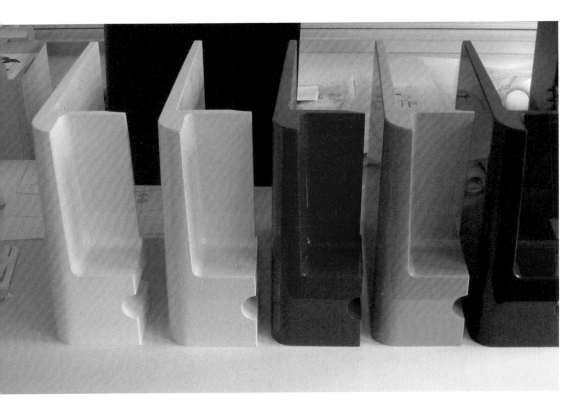

The colors of the replaceable side panels are designed with coffee plantations in mind – where there is sandy earth, blue sky, red coffee berries, green leaves, and brown bean (above top).

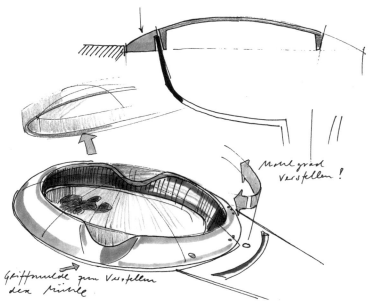

_____ Following a predevelopment stage, in which Jura checked the feasibility of the design and made preliminary models, the machine went to the Swiss company Eugster, an external manufacturer. Candio & Büttler's proposal went up until the design was approved, i.e., until the start of construction. "At that point we didn't even know what the product was called. The name 'Ena' for example only appeared much later and did not come from us," says Büttler. The color concept, the precise choice of material and surface and the different versions of Ena (on the market the cheaper model is Ena 3 and the more expensive one Ena 5) were also decided afterwards.

_____ Because free-form surfaces can best be produced with plastic, Ena primarily consists of that. Thanks to the finish, on the colored side areas the plastic even has the feel of porcelain. Only the cup platforms are made of chrome steel – as are the coffee spouts. Emanuel Probst compares it to the exhaust pipes of a Ferrari: "They too are specially designed to visualize the power of the car."

All you need for a good cup of coffee from the smallest of spaces. Thanks to its trapezoidal shape, the Ena coffee machine looks even more slender.

_____ www.jura.com
_____ www.candiobuettler.ch
_____ Text: Jenny Keller

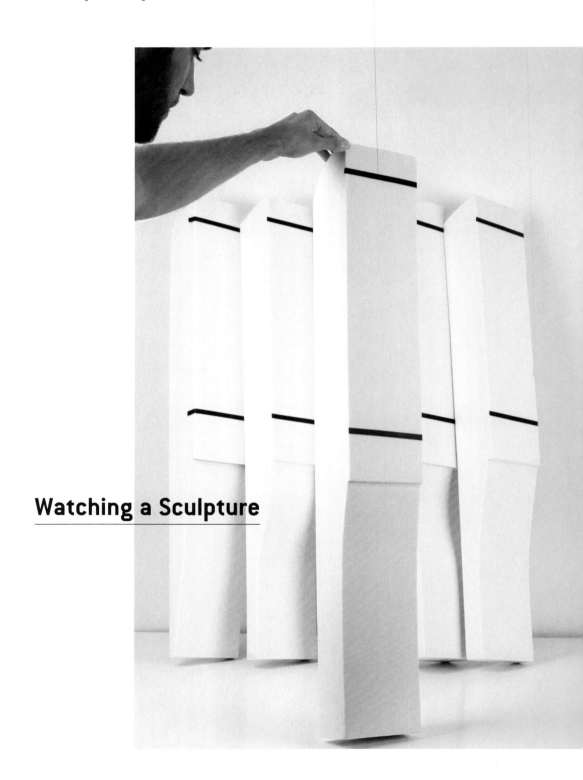

Watching a Sculpture

The Grundig brand is currently redefining itself. With its high-end TV sets it seeks to win back old customers and acquire new ones. One of its first models is the LCD television from the Fine Arts series which it presented at the IFA trade fair in Berlin. The Munich-based Signce Agency designed, among other features, an unusual pattern for the loudspeakers.

_____ Radios and CRT televisions by Grundig – for decades they were part and parcel of millions of German living rooms. The brand stood for the German economic miracle and the reliable quality 'made in Germany'; in fact, back then, there was no foreseeing that anything would change. In the past, the successful recipe of the Nuremberg entertainment electronics group was high-quality mass products at low prices. But at the beginning of the 1980s the concept collapsed – and with it the entire company. Production at its Asian rivals had long since become cheaper. In 2003, Grundig was forced to file for bankruptcy and the Turkish electronics manufacturer Beko and Britain's Alba Group took over the television division, which today operates under the name Grundig Intermedia.

Signce project manager Marco Burkandt sketches different versions of the essentially concave loudspeaker skirting. On the l.: hard foam models of the body.

_____ The brand has only recently started to appear to bounce back, having shed its old tarnished image. New projects in the high-end segment are designed to help Grundig reestablish its name securely alongside other well-known TV makers: These include a new LCD television from the Fine Art series which will be launched in spring next year, and which clearly stands out from the competition. Munich-based design agency Signce (formerly ziba europe) did not receive specific guidelines for the design. "We took the name Fine Arts literally and thought about just what an emotional product can achieve in the relatively sterile field of consumer electronics," says Alf Hackenberg, Creative Director for the project and one of Signce's MDs. Naturally, they didn't have too much scope to play around with as the screen of a flat panel television is fixed. At present, only the loudspeakers have different typologies: They are usually integrated inconspicuously into the housing, but there are also separate, standalone versions. By contrast, the Signce designers chose to use loudspeaker perforation for the expansive fractal decoration that runs along the concave curved aluminum skirt beneath the screen. In a sense it is reminiscent of a crystal or floral pattern, and even has a slightly three-dimensional appearance given the different sizes of the perforation. But Signce disavows any inspiration from nature. "We simply combined various geometrical and ornamental structures," recalls project manager Marco Burkandt. "We were concerned with making a contrast to clear-cut screen surfaces, a tension which the device needs." In addition to the prominent pattern, Signce also presented Grundig with reduced versions featuring conventionally and progressively tapering perforation patterns. The marketing division reacted somewhat skeptically at first, but finally Grundig decided on the free solution after all. "With the other

The loudspeakers are con-
cealed behind the crystalline perforation pattern (below as a sketch). Marco
Burkandt used tape to pinpoint the line of the concave
loudspeaker skirting (be-
low). Left: the designer discussing things with Grundig
design manager Stefanie
Wild and the engineers responsible.

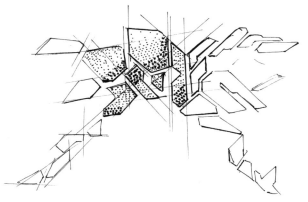

variants the recognition factor was simply missing, they were too flat," says Burkandt. Besides, the unusual pattern suited the Fine Arts model better – Signce has designed it as standalone living sculpture rather than a mere technical appliance. For this reason there are also carefully designed details on the back and bottom of the TV, accentuated by a triple layer of pearl luster paint.

The concave curve and extensive perforation pattern give the Fine Arts TV a striking exterior (below).

_____ The designers had just about three months' time to develop the new model. Grundig wanted to present a cosmetic prototype to the professional public as early as 2006, at the IFA trade fair. The company then needed a further 12 months to move the appliance forward to the point where it could go into mass production. In principle, the TV set remained the way it was in the first design, suggests Burkandt, "and we had that on paper pretty quickly, we didn't have to search for weeks to start with." The set's characteristic elements – such as the visual separation of image and sound or the vertical blue LED element in the loudspeaker skirt – can already be found in the preliminary sketches. Additional Signce projects for Grundig, such as spherical loudspeakers, were also on show at the IFA trade fair.

_____ www.signce.eu
_____ www.grundig.de
_____ Text: Berit Liedtke

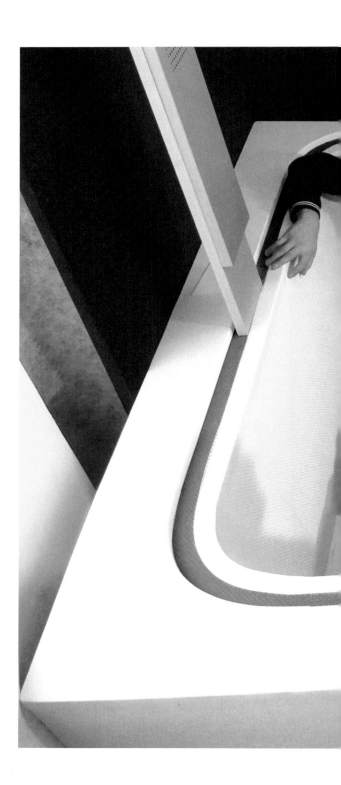

Water on Wheels

The tub's asymmetrical shape is comfortable for both small and large bathers. When you step into the pool, some 50 liters of water spills out, and has to be handled by the overflow.

To get the proportions right there was a lot of experimental bathing in the Hoesch lab (below). The red lines in the CAD rendering outline the radii and transitions for the Italian toolmakers.

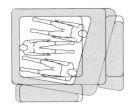

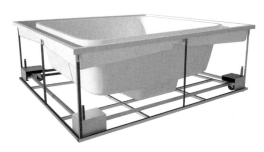

Until now, a whirlpool was a fixed tub intended for use iindoors or outdoors. Now Michael Schmidt from Code 2 Design has given the bubbling tub a fresh interpretation. His creation for Hoesch Design is a piece of furniture on castors you can wheel onto the patio when the sun comes out.

_____ Not only secret agents like James Bond relax in whirlpools. Also known as hot tub or Jacuzzi, the tub, whose powerful jets of water and compressed air massage the skin, can be found in swimming pools, fitness clubs, hotels and cruise ships – and also increasingly in private households. Düren-based Hoesch Design AG and Michael Schmidt from the Stuttgart studio Code 2 Design have showcased a whirlpool on wheels at the 2009 ISH. When empty you can push it from the bathroom onto the patio in the summer. "The portable whirlpool can be used all year round: outside in the summer, and in the house when it is cold and rainy. The same goes for hotels and the like, who cannot afford or do not want two different types of tub," argues Hoesch Sales Director Klaus Marschall. "The pool being portable was not even part of the brief," says Schmidt. In his first sketches he had given the pool an awning because he personally prefers to bathe outdoors, as he did while on vacation in South-East Asia. He presented the sketch to Hoesch Technical Director Jürgen Magin, who responded spontaneously saying: "It must have wheels" – well aware that a full whirlpool can weigh a good 1,200 kilos. However, without water, i.e., a ton lighter, it seemed feasible. Schmidt got in touch with Festo AG in Esslingen. They recommended their bellows cylinders, which, compared with pneumatic, mechanically operated cylinders are relatively hard-wearing. The bellows expand like a tube that you pump air into, and the pool is lifted. That said, a bellows cylinder fills faster, which means the support frame has to remain flexible. The solution was support rollers on the side walls. A similar principle is used in floating piers that are attached to pylons via rollers like the ones Schmidt had seen in Thailand. The patent Code 2 Design and Hoesch apply for will probably be for "portability of large water containers" and have a wide range of applications. Schmidt's original idea was a circular pool. The result was a pool, whose overall shape is asymmetrical. Simultaneously, the pool was to look like a piece of furniture, appear more delicate. The interiors of existing Jacuzzis are shaped like the human body and consequently dictate how occupants can lie or sit in them. "We wanted to find another design that lets you move around more," says Schmidt. Initially, the designers tried with rough sketches and CAD to lower the overall height as much as possible. But when they tested the 1:1 model, made of a wooden structure clad with PU construction panels, it turned out that the sitting area, whose height the designers had adopted from already existing Hoesch pools was not high enough. In the final product it was installed four centimeters higher. Another result of the ergonomics tests in mockup is the world's first whirlpool

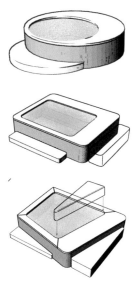

The idea was to give the whirlpool an unusual shape. But how? The early sketches show different asymmetric concepts.

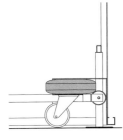

Mobile pool prior to finishing: once the bellows cylinders are filled with compressed air, they expand and thus lift the 200 kg pool. Guiding castors on the sides adjust for differences in height.

hammock, which Hoesch wants to supply as an optional extra. Schmidt: "There are two main positions in the whirlpool, you either lie stretched out or sit – for the jet massage – upright. I want to relax as if floating in the pool, which is how I got the idea of a hammock." It is made of 7.5 millimeter thick 3D mesh, a three-dimensional structure of fabric with a core of fiberglass from Müller Textil in Wiehl. It is elastic and permeable. Reinforced at the edges by means of a welt, the material sags downwards to support the occupant.

_____ Schmidt also got another innovation accepted: an overflow channel on the edge of the pool. This produces a reflecting surface in the pool, and the overflowing water disappears into a narrow groove. With other conventional whirlpools you can either not fill them up to the brim, or they have a mesh channel cover. Even the air from the jets increases the volume by around 20 to 30 liters. Once two people get in they also abruptly displace a further 100 liters. This means the channel has to be large enough so that it can easily handle such amounts of overflowing water. The German DIN standard 19643 allows a width of up to 50 millimeters. Schmidt wanted to make it as narrow as possible. This necessitated experimenting under real conditions in the Hoesch laboratory to find the best solution. The result was an over flow channel 35 millimeters wide with space for a panel with over-flow channel inlet, controls, loudspeaker boxes and freshwater rain showers. The pool also allows Hoesch to demonstrate its know-how with extrusions. The whirlpools are extruded from one piece of polymethylmethacrylate including the overflow channel. The German firm also has a rectangular version in its range for up to five persons: extruding 3,600 by 2,600 millimeters excluding channel from a single piece – that is a real challenge.

_____ www.code2design.de
_____ www.hoesch.de
_____ Text: Katrin Lessing

The asymmetrical Hoesch tub offers more freedom of movement that the custom-ary whirlpools, whose inside tubs tend to be shaped snugly round the body and thus dictate sitting and lying positions.

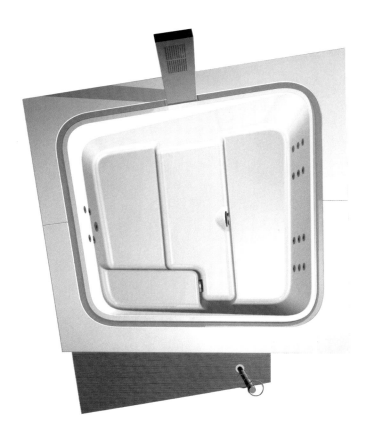

Transportations

Boating Beauty

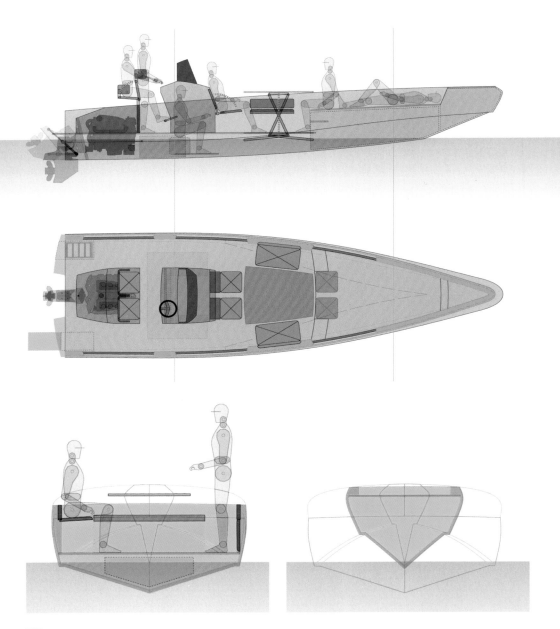

Different user concepts
were developed for the boat,
and then rejected. In a preliminary study, the helm
was placed fully aft with an
area for reclining in front.
Two seats on the side could
simply be folded away (bottom drawing).

Streamlined, fast and light – the Tender 08 motorboat developed by the University of the Applied Sciences of Northwestern Switzerland (FHNW). Thanks to the materials used – fiber compounds the manufacture of which researchers at the Institute for Plastics Technology had vastly improved prior to the design effort. And now Tender 08 hits 43 knots, no problem.

_____ Hard to say why the Swiss have always been so attracted by the seas and the oceans. After all, it was the Helvetian ocean-going fleet that for decades had been the largest of any landlocked country in the world, the largest ship's engines were made in Winterthur for many a year, and the Swiss yacht Alinghi won the America's Cup. And now the Institute for Plastics Technology at the FH Northwestern Switzerland (FHNW)

in Windisch had focused on the subject and developed a new motorboat. There's an ambitious research project lurking behind the striking shape of Tender 08. The goal: to improve the manufacture of fiber compounds. These light and yet durable materials are made up of two main components: reinforcing fibers such as carbon or glass, and a matrix, often made of artificial resin. The way the fibers and resin bond depends mainly on the surface tension of the resin. The research team has now succeeded in optimizing the wetting behavior of the fibers. Tender 08 is the fruit of their labors.

Tender 08 is designed solely for speed – hitting as much as 43 knots. On the inside the motor boat has a minimalist look, from the outside its strange bow shape catches the eye.

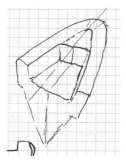

_____ "Engineers are also product developers," affirms project manager Clemens Dransfeld. The Director of the Institute for Plastics Technology is hardly an unknown in the world of boats: with his Dyne Design Engineering office, the engineer and designer was part of the Alinghi design team, and three years ago joined up with Julia Kopp to create the Tender 06 motorboat. Dransfeld now wanted to go one step further. Together with industrial designer Sonja Oswald and engineer Stefan Christ he devoted the best part of two years to the design, which was the implemented by industrial partners, including VW Marine. The result is certainly an eye catcher: while the predecessor model was light and cut a fine figure, the Tender 08 is a whole lot better. "In terms of efficiency, the 08 is far better than its rivals," Dransfeld says. The motorboat is eight meters long, 2.45 meters wide and weighs only 1.6 tons thanks to its lightweight hull. The development, design and construction of the latter were all rolled into one process. Speed forecasts were made, user concepts devised, and ergonomic studies prepared. Using cardboard studies, mock-ups and CAD- as well as CAE models, the team worked on their first main prototype, and then on the tools derived from it. The boat was subsequently built by the Heinrich wharves in Kreuzlingen. The most striking design element is the strangely double-notched bows. It takes its cue from classical yachts as well as from flying boats from

Dry run: Clemens Dransfeld and Sonja Oswald (left) from FHNW developed the design using card models and mock-ups. The infusion process for the compounds was then transferred onto sections (below) moving from lab scale to life size.

The boat uses a modular concept: the inner shell can be inserted completely into the hull and glued in place (top). The original model was milled to later be used as a mold for the tool molds (above and right).

Light and sharp: For the Tender 08, improved fiber compound structures were tested for the first time on a real-life product. They feature two main components: the reinforcing fibers and a matrix of artificial resins. The researchers have managed to optimize the fibers´ wetting characteristics.

the animated cartoons of Japan's Hayao Miyazaki. Apart from that, the boat is characterized by clean lines and the combination of gleaming green-lacquered high-tech structures and a traditional teak deck. The Tender 08's interior can accommodate up to eight people, and is very minimal and uncluttered in appearance. There are six chairs for that great picnic in the bay, and two side seats flip up after use and the table stows away. Two large reclining areas on the forward deck and over the engine room will appeal to the sunbathers. "We had to calculate things down to the very last millimeter to create such comforts," Dransfeld reports. The boat promises to offer fast 43 knot fun: the TDI 225-6 engine delivers 225 horsepower and it is the latest VW Marine development. The engine's output and peak rpm-performance enable Tender 08 to swiftly get up to speed and it handles curves superbly. At full throttle: at the water sports trade fair Boot in January, Tender 08 caused a real stir, and two of the three boats already built have sold for 220,000 Swiss francs each. Another sector has also pricked up its ears: there is talk of the FHNW now following things up with a project for the aerospace industry.

_____ www.fhnw.ch
_____ Text: Andrea Eschbach
_____ Fotos: Martin Hemmi und FHNW
_____ Illustrations: Dani Scherrer

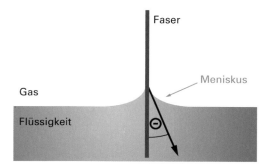

Faser

Meniskus

Gas

Flüssigkeit

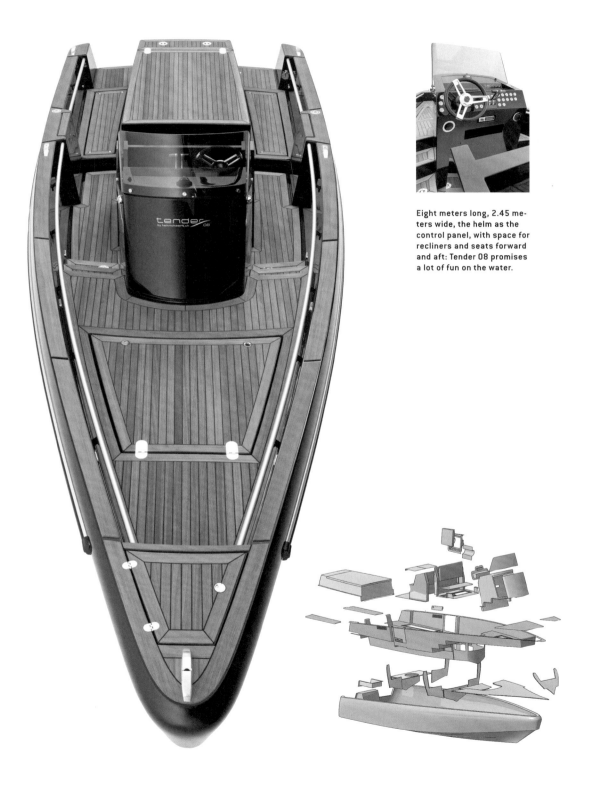

Eight meters long, 2.45 meters wide, the helm as the control panel, with space for recliners and seats forward and aft: Tender 08 promises a lot of fun on the water.

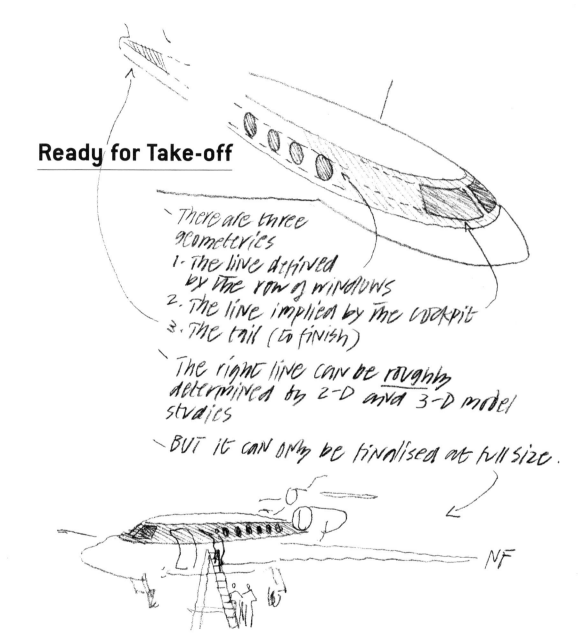

Ready for Take-off

There are three
geometries
1. The line derived
by the row of windows
2. The line implied by the cockpit
3. The tail (to finish)

The right line can be roughly
determined by 2-D and 3-D model
studies

BUT it can only be finalised at full size.

NF

Designing an aircraft is something many designers dream of – but the task is still often left up to engineers. Star architect Norman Foster, at least, was able to design not just the interior of 33 business jets for the Netjets Europe airline, he also lent them a striking graphic appearance.

For Norman Foster (above) a dream was fulfilled. He designed not only the airplane interior for Netjets Europe, but a new outer paint job, too. The blue strip that runs from the cockpit to the end of the fuselage is reminiscent of the CI of Lufthansa that Otl Aicher created back in the 1980s.

_____ Norman Foster is a passionate pilot. "The romantic idea of flying has a hold on me," says the 73-year-old star architect. "The airplane, this body in space, seemingly weightless, independent of everything, completely its own system, is something which fascinates me." Indeed, one can discern allusions to aircraft construction in many of Foster's buildings, one prime example being the Swiss Re Center in London. He has already designed a number of airports, most recently the one in Beijing, which can all be traced back to Berlin Tempelhof, the "mother of all airports" in his eyes. But never an airplane. This is still a matter for engineers. But it remains the dream project of many designers, who are generally only consulted when it comes to the interior.

_____ In fact, Foster's task was also to only design the interior of 33 new Falcon 7X business jets, which airline company Netjets Europe ordered from French aircraft builder Dassault. Or so it was thought, until he realized that the graphics on the fuselage did not really suit his client, who had now become by far the largest operator of business jets in Europe, flying its customers to, for example, European Cup soccer matches and Art Basel. Leaving all graphicical gimmicks aside, he added a striking dark blue stripe which unites the cockpit and cabin windows and extends all the way to the tail. It looks classic, almost retro. And not entirely by coincidence it resembles the famous dark blue of Lufthansa's logo, which Foster's long-deceased friend Otl Aicher designed in the 1960s.

_____ "For many years we didn't take design so seriously," admits Graeme Weston, Chief Operating Officer at Netjets. But now Foster has convinced them, he says. "The jets with the blue stripe are instantly recognizable," according to Weston. And for this reason the new design is to feature on all 160 airplanes in the Netjets fleet. In the interior as well, Foster was not concerned with displaying luxury. You won't find any golden surfaces, pink kitsch or dark burl wood here. Instead, there are functional, clearly separated areas: The dark, cool galley dominated by carbon fiber surfaces and the light cabin completely lined with both real and synthetic leather which accommodates up to 13 people. Passengers pass through a narrow dark corridor into a bright, spacious room which intensifies the effect.

_____ "My definition of comfort is to have the luxury of choice," says Foster. Here in the cabin you should be able to remain undisturbed – perforated leather highlights the fact that this is a relaxation zone and the chairs can easily be converted into beds. But you should be able to use the room just as easily to work in, as Norman Foster himself often does while

Passengers enter the spacious cabins via a dark, carbon-fiber-clad corridor (left). The toilet has elm/maple paneling (below), and even on the outside the jet looks elegant thanks to the new paint job (bottom).

supervising projects worldwide. "If I want to work with a number of people from my team around a table and prepare a presentation, this has to be possible in an airplane." What is also important is "the catering for the extremes of community and privacy." Thus additional seating can be folded out, the fiddleback maple veneer tables can be extended at any time, headrests can be made to disappear. Sometimes it is just details which Norman Foster has redesigned a little. For example, that the gap from which the ceiling is indirectly lit also functions as a handhold – passengers will thank him if they are standing when the aircraft encounters turbulence.

_____ www.fosterandpartners.com
_____ www.netjets.com
_____ Text: Markus Zehentbauer

The cabin is completely covered in different types of both real and artificial leather. All the furniture is so flexible that you can enjoy working or sleeping in one and the same seat.

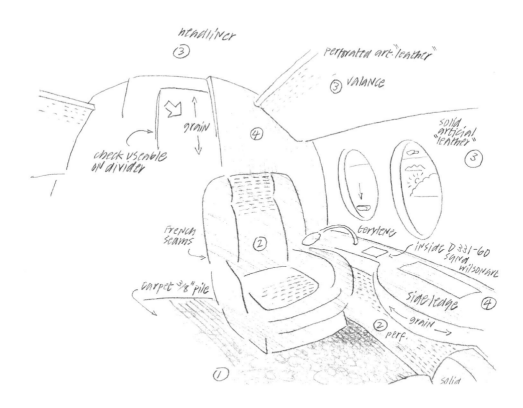

The Model With a Cause

Most motor scooters today look either overly dynamic or nostalgic – not so the version created by Dutch office GRO Design: It goes completely for simplified forms and it's this that catches the eye.

_____ Since its foundation in the late nineties, the Eindhoven-based studio GRO Design produces a design study once a year on a topic that it chooses for itself. The idea behind is that "we want to tackle new product categories and thus develop new clients," state Roger Swales and Roland Bird, founding members of the company and formerly designers at Philips. The latest project: the Scoot electric scooter, a vehicle study developed in cooperation with TIM modelmakers. The scooter will go on its travels this year in the form of a presentation model, touring Milan, New York and London. A brief glance at the drawings shows that the scooter takes up the archetypal characteristics of the traditional Vespa as produced by Piaggio, and combines this with a highly simplified repertoire of shapes. The project was informed by the twin notions of style and simplicity, the wish to reduce-to-the-max and the re-emergence of the Ulm canon on radii. Swales summarizes the project as "It's all about reduction." The clear and simple shapes foster a striking symbol. The design's identity, so Bird suggests, can be seen from the back: soft edges uphold the open structure of the overall shape and address the modern iPod generation. For all the simplicity, it is hard to pinpoint the Scoot in terms of formal aesthetic properties. The close affinities to household appliances and communication products may initially irritate the eye – even at second glance! The reason: the design process, which is typical for industrial design. The initial focus was on exploring the product segment: scenarios were devised to position the new object in our everyday world. Then any number of sketches and card models followed; finally the shape chosen was given a virtual existence using Rhino software package. At the end of the design process a presentation model was built, relying not only on digital data and on computer-aided methods, but also on the expertise of a model builder.

_____ This is a customary approach in industrial design – but is definitely unusual in transportation design. In Scoot's case, GRO made use of processes typical for designing appliances – but what they came up with this time was not a coffee machine, but a vehicle. This is evidenced by the very first sketches for the Scoot. Unlike the usual, strongly exaggerated, dynamically distorted representations that auto designers tend to come up with, the drawings seem prosaic and almost naive. Both the overall form and the intrinsic structural composition of the concept scooter are constructed in two dimensions, and then culminate in detailed graphic features. This description could be applied to all the objects designed by GRO. "We generally work with pronounced graphic lines," reports Swales. Lines that tend to give the Scoot the appearance that it is standing still, not driving. And the

For their design of an electric roller, the GRO designers looked to role models such as the Vespa. Top: a diamond-shaped structure is intended to decrease slippage on the footboard.

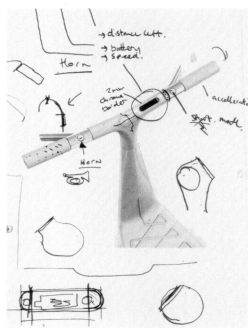

GRO Design's sketches and models have nothing to do with the dynamically warped representations we are familiar with from transportation design, rather, they are rooted in industrial design.

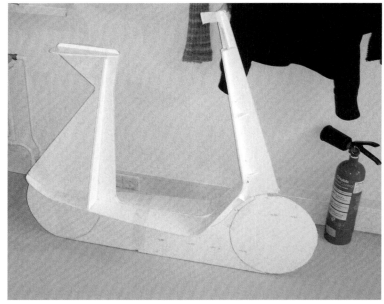

treatment of the surfaces between the lines also sets the electronic vehicle apart from its current mechanical compatriots. Developing highly complex surface geometries is a task that involves immense amounts of input and in-depth experience in auto design. But GRO took a completely different path. It is still unclear whether the study will ever go into series production. The search for a suitable partner is on. "The next step would be to produce functioning prototypes for riding trials," says Swales, who concedes that the design would probably have to undergo a few changes before it can be produced. Perhaps one day we'll be greeted on the street by a Scoot. An exciting prospect!

_____www.grodesign.com
_____ Text: Melanie Kurz

A Clever Concept

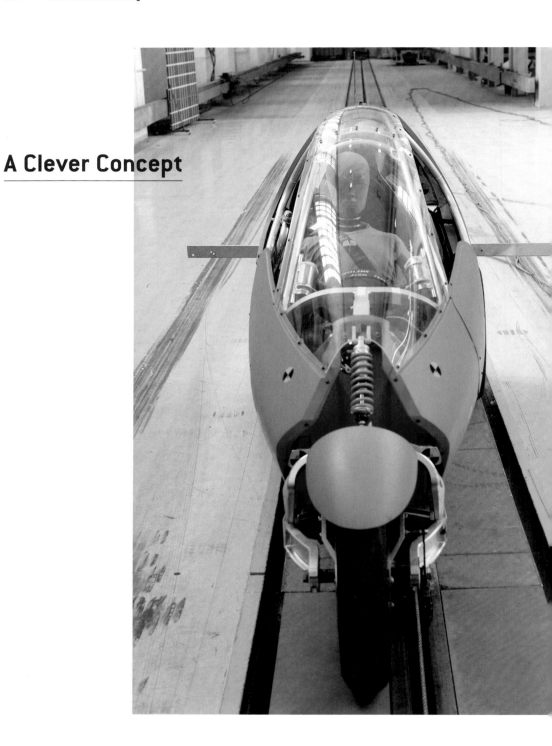

Pioneering concepts for vehicles are typically born behind the closed doors of automobile corporations – and after their presentation at trade fairs disappear into the archives again. But that need not be the case, as the Clever trike demonstrates. Munich-based designer Peter Naumann lets us in on the design process behind the two-seater urban vehicle.

_____ Drive and save: a rare motto in the age of city-bound SUVs that move through traffic like battleships. The compact, low-emission vehicle for urban transport called Clever was designed to provide something missing to date in low-energy vehicles, namely driving pleasure. Anyone on the road in one of the prototypes has the impression that they are riding a motorbike. Except that in this case it is not the driver who determines the tilt but the on-board computer. The Clever's narrow wheels mean that the three-wheeler leans into the bend – thanks to a fully-automatic hydraulic system. It is fitted with a conventional steering wheel. Created by designer Peter Naumann, the vehicle consumes as little as three liters per 100 kilometers. It is not conceived as a pared-down micro car or a hyped up motorbike. Clever unites two worlds: it handles like a motorbike, yet delivers almost the same comfort and safety of an automobile. Furthermore, it possesses an essential quality, namely mobility. It can escape congestion and slots into even the smallest parking space.

_____ In Naumann's design studio in Munich, a rocket on three wheels shoots across the screen on fat tires. The taillights glow. A futuristic vehicle, representing the embodiment of speed and agility. Naumann grins: "That was what sparked the whole thing off, the start. Naturally exaggerated like in a comic." And yet his first sketches included all the features he wanted for the vehicle. It was while drawing and rendering that he realized how Clever could work. The driver section and engine block had to be separated. Like a pod, the capsule for driver and passenger extends out over the bulky outboard engine that does not, at first sight, look gas-fueled. The single-cylinder 213 cubic centimeters CNG motor produces 15 HP, meaning the vehicle can accelerate from 0 to 60 kilometers per hour in less than seven seconds – more than sufficient for urban trips. That said, it cannot top 100 kilometers per hour. It is fitted with two removable gas bottles, which can also be replaced at gas stations and supermarkets, should there not be an LPG station close-by. If you trace the design process, the Clever chronology reads like a textbook example of a design approach frequently preached yet seldom achieved: venture something new and implement it quickly. Since 2002, the Institute for Vehicles at the TU Berlin has led a European consortium of research institutes with the aim to produce an "environmentally friendly, low-cost urban vehicle." The brief sounded daring: half the fuel consumption of the Smart and half its width. Such reductions can only be achieved using cutting-edge technologies. Peter Naumann's Clever unites

Safe narrow-gauge vehicle: during the crash test on the grounds of TU Berlin (left) Clever did as well as a normal compact car.

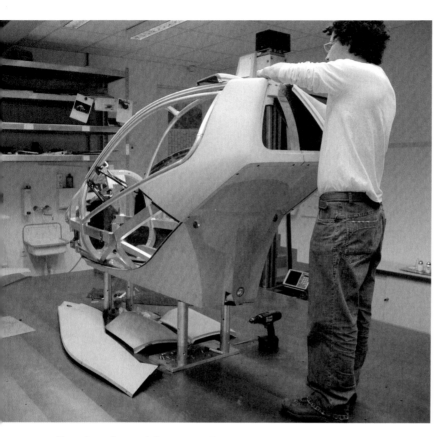

Above: Australian specialist Marco Rech filling and sanding the prototype's fiberglass-reinforced plastic shell. Peter Naumann and his team also developed new tire profiles and hubs (right): The front uses motorcycle tires, the back car tires.

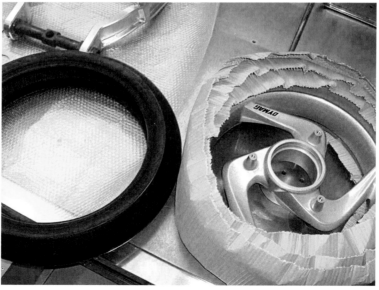

a minimum traffic surface and minimum weight. In fact, automakers had already abandoned the idea of a three-wheeler scooter-plus-cab back in the 1950s. But this re-working has nothing in common with the boneshaking vehicles produced then. The streamlined vehicle weighs in at just 400 kilograms, is around one meter wide and three meters long; aluminum spaceframe, plastic chassis and natural gas motor lower fuel consumption further to 2.6 liters per 100 kilometers.

_____ When BMW joined the project as cooperation partner, things began to take on shape. A design competition was organized between four studios, which Naumann's office won – less than three years remained in which to complete the project. It was to the designer's advantage that he had already worked on several motorbikes. "You only have one shot in such projects," he says, and it must hit the target. His concept located the cabin over the engine, foresaw a streamlined outline and relied on gas as fuel source. Initially he managed without detailed physical models. Everything was computer-generated. The experienced professor of Industrial Design at the University of Applied Sciences in Munich, Germany, sent BMW a set of D data. "This meant it was possible to supply the engineers with the data in a very short space of time," he recalls. The engineering boffins at BMW were then "immediately able to check" the chassis data. Though the bodywork was altered in consultation with the engineers, it never lost its basic dynamic shape. Then, at long last, everything was ready to roll. Naumann Design presented a first 1-in-4 scale model produced using the rapid prototyping technique. The project was well received. By the end of the year all the components and the first prototypes for driving tests had been built. Then the

The automatic tilt control ensures a pleasurable ride (above). Should Clever go into production, then it will be registered as a motorbike that you can drive using a car license. Below: Peter Naumann, Thorsten Bergmaier and Roberto Maronde (from left to right) discussing designs.

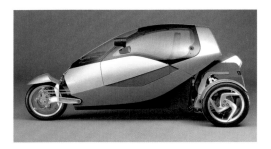

Aerodynamic tricycle: From the front, the Clever prototype looks like the cockpit of a jet plane. The wing door is only on the left.

moment of truth arrived. A number of crash tests had to show whether the cabins met all expectations. The frame delivered what the digital data promised: Three stars in the EuroNCAP Test matched the rating for a runabout. Compared with conventional vehicles the low vehicle width and soft contours reduces the damage in accidents involving pedestrians. Then, the first roadworthy prototype was built by PSW Automotive Engineering GmbH in Ingolstadt, Germany. The EU Commission, which had supported the pioneering project from the start was very enthusiastic. Peter Naumann put the car through its paces, two months later work was done on a second prototype with an electric drive, which was scheduled to be completed within a few weeks. The tilting three-wheeler with the tandem-style seats has what it takes to be a great success. Industrial production has definitely not been ruled out.

_____ www.naumann-design.de
_____ Text: Oliver Herwig

Experiments

The Making of Pixeleyu

Rolling, Rolling, Rolling!

With the Pixelroller by London-based design collective Random International Ltd., digital images and text can actually be rolled onto the wall. Alongside appearances put in with the hand-held printing tool all over the world, the young designers are busy readying the prototype for the market.

_____ A white wall, a laptop and a rod-like tool with a roller fixed onto the end that looks like a perfectly normal paint roller: That is, it would if there were no cables coming from the laptop, disappearing into an opening in the bottom of the handle and emerging again at the top at a sort of print head. They immediately bring to mind the transfer of digital data. Thus the novel tool with a familiar form is called the Pixelroller, and the laptop contains a software program written by Stuart Wood during his MA course at the Royal College of Art in London. His college friend Florian Ortkrass developed the output device for it. But how does it work? Ortkrass starts rolling the device up and down on the wall with generous strokes. The print head runs easily on two metal wheels, leaving behind black paint, but it does not cover the surface completely like a conventional paint roller, only certain spots. Gradually, the lines of color and blank areas form one complete motif. It barely takes a minute for the motif to be finished. The process remotely recalls the scratching of a lottery card. In reality, the pixel-based image is scanned and then reproduced with a short time delay by digitally-controlled stamp rolls running parallel to each other. The stamp rolls are fed with ink from paint jets; wherever no application of color is required, individual rolls are retracted whilst the remaining ones continue running over the wall surface. In contrast to linear scanning, where, like a copier, the entire width of the image is scanned and the vertical axis is gradually built up, here the scanning process is started by the user.

It looks like a paint roller, but functions like a hand-held printer: With the Pixel-roller you can transfer digi-tal images and text onto large areas. Here, Stuart Wood of Random Interna-tional is rolling the heading for this article onto the studio wall.

Stuart Wood, Hannes Koch and Florian Ortkrass (from left) founded the collective Random International Ltd. in 2002 while still studying Product Design at Brunel University in London. Their most complex project to date is the Pixelroller. They have developed two methods to transfer the paint to the wall – it is either printed with a stamp roller or sprayed on. Below left: Design for the stamp roller's automatic paint supply.

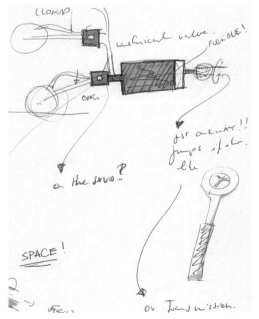

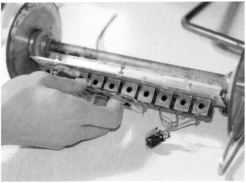

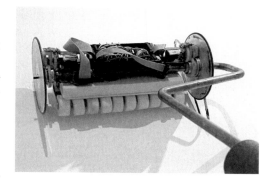

_____ Hannes Koch, who has been part of the design collective with Wood and Ortkrass since 2002, compares the function with the movement of the mouse: "Scanning begins the moment you start rolling", he says. "The software is program-med so that scanning always begins in the center of the image, and not in the bottom left-hand corner, for example." Everything else, i.e., speed and movement, is left to the user to decide. "The delay between scanning and printing is like the minimal delay we see with the cursor on a com-puter screen when we move the mouse," according to Koch. But the impor-tant thing, he adds, is not to roll too quickly, for "then the mechanisms go on strike." In other words, the stamp rolls cannot keep pace. Color intensity decreases and the motif is elongated, as when you pull a piece of paper through a printer as it is still printing.

_____ The three designers are proud of the rendering quality of the cur-rent prototype. This may seem odd when we consider the blocky, single-color motifs. However, you need to have seen its predecessors. Since the first attempts, which began with a light roller for photosensitive paper and led to Ortkrass and Wood's joint thesis, the designers have been constantly improving and refining the highest possible resolution with ever smaller image formats. They have already halved the printing surface compared to the first prototype: at present the smallest portrait that is still recognizable is A2 size. They are currently experimenting with paint from spray cans, with which they want to increase the number of paint jets from 17 to 24 while keeping the width of the roller the same. The advantage of spray can paint over the water-soluble paint they used up to this point, is its lower viscosity, which also makes it suitable for smaller valves. Special valves at the spray cans allow the color to be sprayed directly onto the wall via paint jets – without any physical contact with the surface. To be fit for the market – and the designers agree on this – the device has to be even smaller with a still higher resolution and wireless option.

This prototype works with digitally controlled stamp rollers which are continu-ously fed ink from tins of paint. Where no paint is required, individual rollers are drawn in mechanically while the rest of the rollers remain in contact with the surface of the wall.

_____ However, they happily leave the battle of the most pixels and high-est resolutions to the image industry: "We don't regard the Pixelroller in the same category as conventional printers, which have to satisfy demands for photorealistic images", says Koch. They are all much more interested in the very individual aesthetics of their hand-held printer and the ever-new pos-sibilities for use they discover with the innovative roller and various spin-offs – whether for Nokia, light designer Ingo Maurer or British department store Selfridges. Besides making digital data visible, the Pixelroller makes unique works out of endlessly reproducible motifs. The best example is the pixelography of a portrait of Ingo Maurer, which the designers rolled with

The designers rolled out
the portrait of Ingo Maurer
in the darkroom with a light
roller, an early version of
the Pixelroller. They call
individual works like this
pixelography.

the light roller in the dark room and subsequently exposed. This unconventional way of handling digital data has also lately been practiced by Swiss Jürg Lehni, whose spray-can installation Hektor can plot vector graphics. You may want to take a look at his way of vizualizing things at the website www.hektor.ch, especially the video section is worth a visit, showing the truely astonishing process of a ghostly moving spray-can drawing conclusions on the wall. However, the form in which the Pixelroller will one day come onto the market depends on the future manufacturer. With their business unit Operation Schoener Ltd., the designers are already in talks with interested parties in the industry. In analogy to the good old paint roller, they definitely want to stick to the tool's archetypal form.

_____ www.random-international.com
_____ Text: Karianne Fogelberg

The starting point of the Pixelroller project was a light roller which draws on light-sensitive surfaces with LEDs. Above: Different versions; the LED painting pen is a spin-off ready to be launched on the market.

A Well-Tempered Project

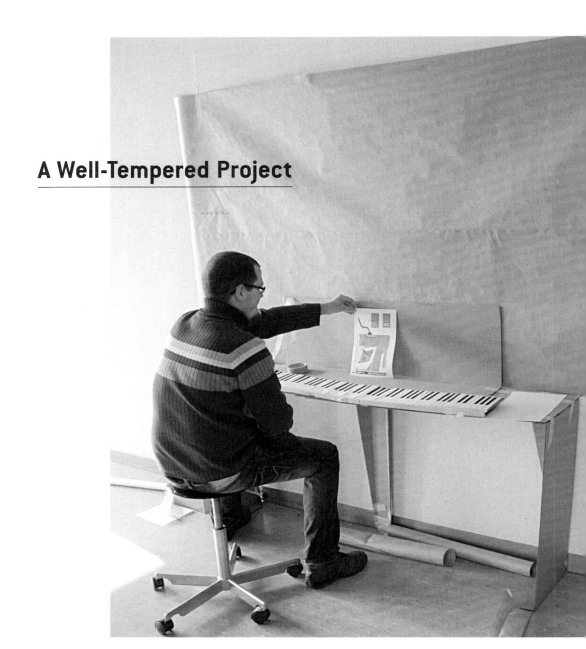

Two Swiss enthusiasts have reinvented the digital piano: industrial designers Daniel Schär and Karin Heinrich have developed a system that combines the advantages of an electric piano with those of its acoustic sibling. They have called their instrument the Elodie, and it not only sounds better than the usual electric piano, but looks better, too.

_____ It could easily be just a normal sideboard. 1.4 meters wide, 75 centimeters high, with a black lacquer finish, and straight lines. On the wall next to it hang two white panels, perhaps an abstract work of art. Yet if you open the top of the sideboard, you find yourself gazing at a keyboard, and if you tap one of the keys the surface starts to resonate. What looked like a piece of furniture is actually an electronic piano – an instrument that seldom catches the eye with its elegant appeal. "We wanted our design to stand out firmly from the conservative mainstream. We are of the opinion that, as regards the design, there is a massive amount of scope for action – precisely in the case of electric pianos, as the technology differs from the complex structure of an acoustic instrument in that it offers great scope for design experiments," comments Daniel Schär (27). Together with Karin Heinrich (37) the industrial designer then developed Elodie, the new vibra-acoustic digital piano – as their graduation project at Northwest Switzerland's University of the Applied Sciences (FHNW) in Aarau. The two design students had four months to develop the new product. And numerous extensive acoustic experiments, countless sketches, and various models were first necessary before they agreed on the futurist, yet restrained, design. The hardest part, they recall, was developing a logical overall concept.

Karin Heinrich (above) and Daniel Schär (left-hand page) have come up with the first vibra-acoustic digital piano with mobile sounding boards: Elodie is surely as practical as a digital piano and sounds as good as an acoustic piano.

_____ So, what to do? Create a portable piano that could be assembled from various parts or an iPod piano that could be used to download notes? A hybrid of piano and grand piano, or a street vibra-piano that could be placed on walls and other surfaces to be played? "After an awful lot of talking we finally decided against the more spacy, nerdy instrument version," Karin Heinrich says. Alongside the aesthetic criteria, acoustics played a key part in the thinking: "Primarily, the instrument has to meet the musician's needs and we therefore did not want to devise some off-beat thing that had a certain sound, but rather a piano that sounded as good as a piano," Heinrich continues – she trained in piano building. The result: the first vibra-acoustic digital piano with a mobile sounding board – and it comes pretty close to emulating the sound of an acoustic piano.

_____ The designers had the idea for it, so they say, by chance. Hans Peter Gutjahr, a sound technician and head of the FHNW's sound studio, advised the two students on acoustic matters. And it was he who drew their attention to magnet vibrator technology (Soliddrive), namely a vibrating loudspeaker that needs no membrane, and which can be fastened to tables, display windows and other flat surfaces and causes the material on which it is

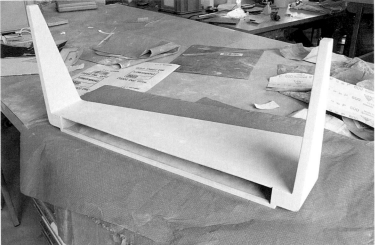

The designers initially wanted to produce a piano that stands against the wall like conventional pianos (top left). They then decided on a less static version. Left: the shape is reminiscent of a grand piano.

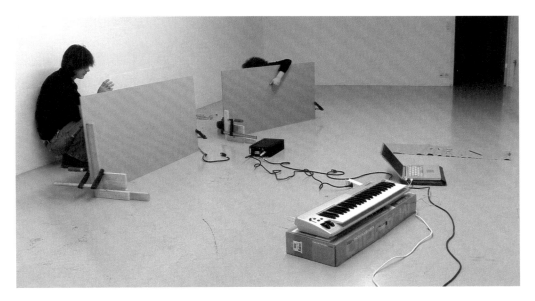

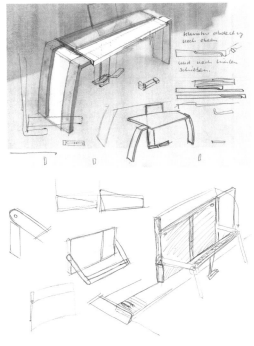

Top: Tests with an USB keyboard, with the sound being
produced via computer,
amplifier and the sounding
boards. After testing a
number of materials they
found out that wood com-
bined with aluminum pro-
duced the best sound.

The sounding boards float freely and are connected to the frame construction and technical components such as the amplifier and the solid drive technology. The aluminum board is 1.5 mm thin and the air-ply board 4 mm.

fastened to resonate – turning the entire surface into a loudspeaker. This surface sound converter technology has now been on the market for a good five years and so is not exactly new, but the designer duo immediately sensed that it was the right one for their project. After all, the loudspeakers had actually been the starting point of the graduation project, because the loudspeaker technology that enables the sonic qualities of an acoustic piano to be coupled with the advantages of a digital piano – lightness, mobility, and price. In the classic acoustic piano, a piano wire is struck by a felt hammer and its oscillations conducted via the frame onto the wooden sounding board, from where they spread out in space. The principle behind the sound created by the vibra-acoustic digital piano is similar, but here the electromagnetic loudspeaker boxes take on the role of the striking hammer and the oscillating wire. The sound waves are thus not disseminated via a sounding board inside the instrument but by the surface to which the loudspeakers are attached. "Our first tests with the loudspeakers were very amusing and impressive. For example, we fastened them to a table that then vibrated so strongly that it started moving around the room. It was as if the table was the actual source of the sound!" recalls Daniel Schär.

_____ Together with audio technician Hans Peter Gutjahr, the students had to find out what supporting materials most sounded like a real piano. Plaster or PVC, aluminum or wood? Each material creates its own characteristic timbre. "Plaster, for example, creates a huge echo. And in general it was the high tones that were problematic, as in most cases they did not sound clear or loud enough," Karin Heinrich adds. After countless trials in the sound studio it transpired that a combination of two materials best imitated the range of sounds of a piano – namely aluminum and plywood, used in airplanes. The two resonating panels for the digital piano can either be hung on the wall or placed on the floor. Each oscillates freely in a frame structure and is linked with the technical components such as the amplifier and the SolidDrive loudspeakers. The sonic experience then depends on the positioning of the mobile, modular sounding panels in the particular room – this is restricted by the length of the cable connecting the piano to the loudspeakers. If the cable is more than 4m long, then the sound gets distorted. With an Elodie you don't just play digital piano – you play on and with the room you are in. And if you don't want this fun side to things, then you can opt to simply play your Elodie like a ordinary digital piano, using ordinary earphones …

_____ www.danielschaer.ch
_____ Text: Katharina Altemeier

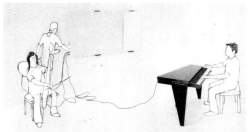  

Elodie can be placed any-where in the room. The sounding boards either hang down the wall or stand on the floor. Additional musical instruments can also be connected up (top left).

Jerszy the Dripper

The furniture designed by Jerszy Seymour was the most off-beat of the exhibits in a show called "MyHome – Seven Experiments for a new Way of Living" that was presented at the Vitra Design Museum: colorfully dyed one-off items that have nothing in common with what rapid prototyping machines and CNC milling machines are turning out at the moment. Jerszy Seymour has a vision – namely that at some point in the future everyone will be able to produce furniture in their own kitchen – made simply from grated potatoes.

_____ "You can probably sit on them somehow, but they are not really made for that purpose," Jerszy Seymour says commenting on his first prototypes for Living Systems, which he sent from his design studio in Berlin to Weil am Rhein. The sculptures look like colorful icing without a cake underneath, and double up as furniture: a bed, a table, a chair, and arm-chair and a lampshade. Seymour made them from starch-based thermoplastic, derived from ordinary potatoes. He spent two months experimenting in empty premises he rented specially for the purpose. And even if the initial products from the hand-made material are still far too brittle, the trials were so promising that Seymour is already planning an entire series made of bio-plastic. Seymour is still keeping the mixture a secret: he does reveal that he went shopping in a supermarket. Alongside potatoes he used milk and alcohol, and then colored the mix with food coloring at the end. The individual elements of the plastic mixture are easy to handle, but the difficulty is doing the right thing at the right time when making the plastic mix: Seymour mixes the grated potatoes with distilled water, and then he filters and dries them to extract the starch. He heats the flakes with milk and the mixture ferment owing to the reaction of the bacteria with the lactic acid. He then centrifuges and condenses everything, until he gets a polymer as the final product.

The thermoplastic looks like bright sugar coating. Left page: Seymour's Assistant Stephane Barbier-Bouvet applies the mixture, using a grease gun. Below: Jerszy Seymour (*1968)

_____ In the Vitra Design Museum, Seymour has demonstratively staged his Living Systems as a process, with potato plants, milk bottles, a trestle table with hotplates and crusted pots, and, last but not least, sand, which he uses as a mold for the furniture. Stéphane Barbier-Bouvet, Seymour's assistant, who handled most of the experiments, initially attempted to pour the plastic directly from the pot onto the sand molds, then switched to a funnel and did it as if he were Jackson Pollock dripping. "We then tried to build our own kind of injection molding machine. The hardest thing was the screw that transports the mixture, and we had to abandon the idea." In the final instance they used a grease gun such as can be bought in a car parts store. The mixture was heated in a pot, filled into the gun and then squeezed out. Initially, the plastic still spilled out of the mold, because the material contracts by about five percent when hardening, and the joints between the horizontal levels and the edges of the sand molds cracked. In the next

Experimental kitchen: The bio-plastic is made of potatoes, milk, alcohol and food dyes. The recipe may be simple, but the manufacturing is tough — Seymour is constantly working to improve it.

Using the prepared sand molds, the bio-plastic is then used to form furniture (below). The sand has binder added to deliver the right rigidity.

In the Vitra Design Museum Seymour showed how furniture production could be a DIY trip – with an installation entitled Living Systems. His vision: anyone can mold their own furniture using ingredients from the supermarket. The bio-plastic is still too brittle and the process still too complicated for anyone to use it.

trials, Seymour and his assistants therefore first created the horizontal surfaces and then squirted the connections to the base. The experiments were preceded by several months of research. Seymour talked to engineers and found out that the plastics which the major producers market as "biodegradable" are nevertheless produced from petroleum. He wanted, at any rate, to use raw materials for the Living Systems that could be manufactured in a pre-industrial and fully self-sufficient manner. The materials are only one aspect of his project as "plastics made of regenerative materials are not exactly spectacular in the design world and in five years' time everyone will have biologically degradable plastics in their lines. The focus must also be on establishing a personal relationship to the objects, investing in a piece of furniture in order to appropriate and keep it." Seymour wants to visualize the processes of design production, distribution and consumption – and with the Vitra installation he also tells the story of the potato as a critique of capitalism.

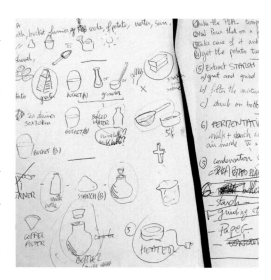

For two months Jerszey Seymour experimented in an empty room he rented specially for the purpose – and countless sketches arose in the process.

_____ www.jerszyseymour.com
_____ www.design-museum.de
_____ Text: Cornelia Durka

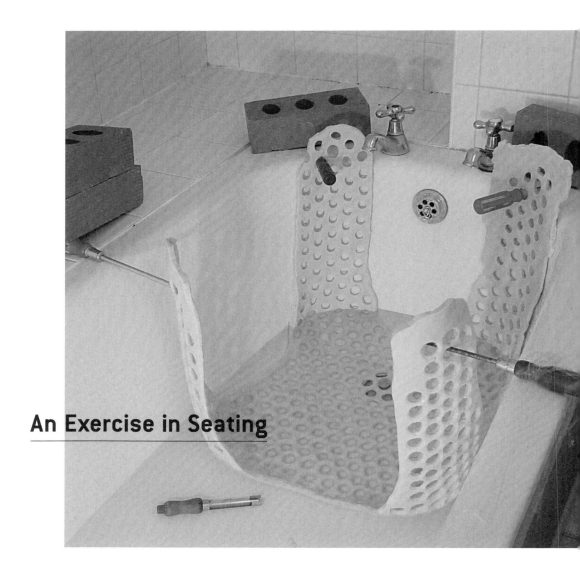

An Exercise in Seating

"Exercises in Seating" is the title of a series of chairs which RCA graduate Max Lamb has derived from unusual materials and experimental production techniques. The results of his investigation have been presented in the Design Mart exhibition at the London Design Museum. Here he recounts his most difficult case, a stool made of nanocrystalline copper.

_____ My initial intention for utilising the electro-deposition process was to produce a chair in expanded polystyrene. Yet, an early experiment with Ross Morgan of Morganic Metal Ltd. did not display the required material characteristics. The conductive silver solution that I carefully sprayed onto the object has an alcohol base that corrodes styrene. And the polystyrene model was too light and buoyant to be submerged in the electro-deposition tank. Having discounted polystyrene, I discovered a type of modelling wax produced by British Wax that is very rigid at room temperature, yet at temperatures above 40 to 50 degree becomes easily manipulable by hand. Best of all, the wax can be melted from the copper shell once electro-deposited, and reused for new models.

Max Lamb has no problem with using materials and production processes thought to have been lost: At the top we see him at his local beach in Cornwall, casting a three-legged stool out of lead. For his unique copper stool he forms modeling wax in the bathtub and cuts out the pattern of holes with an apple corer.

_____ I began modelling the wax using my bath filled with hot water. My first full sized chair was, from memory, a hand-made replica of Gio Ponti's Superleggera chair of 1957. I chose this chair due to its structural integrity and amazing lightness. My wax Superleggera was incredibly difficult to construct, due to the size of my bath. I had to build the chair in seven sections and then join them once out of the bath by heating the joint area locally using a hairdryer. Though I liked the handmade, naïve character of the chair I encountered structural problems. The delicacy of the legs and uprights of the backrest could not support the heavy wax, and very gradually the chair began to slump. This could be disastrous when in the electro-deposition tank.

_____ So I proceeded to make a four-legged stool in thick sheets of wax, with a pattern of holes for visual lightness and additional rigidity. I rolled out a 15 millimeter-thick sheet of wax in the bath with a rolling pin. With an old apple corer I cut regularly spaced holes into the wax and I created legs using the tap end of the bath as a mold. I ended up with an oblong stool with four gently curving legs, entirely covered in a pattern of circular holes. I carefully removed the structure from the bath and began to carve a chamfer around all of the holes. With over 400 holes this was a time consuming process. At this stage I realised that to smooth the top surface I had to submerge the entire stool in hot water again. But the water I placed it in was slightly too hot and upon near completion of my laboriously carved wax stool, just

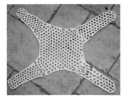

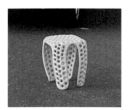

The perforation is intended to make the stool lighter and ensure it is stable. To round off the perforated edges smoothly, the wax model has to be dipped in hot water – but not too hot. Above: the wax model, melted by water that was too hot.

one hour prior to delivering it to Morganic Metal for copper encapsulation, the structure melted. My stool was irretrievably slumped at the bottom of my bath. Three hours of sleep and a cup of tea later, I started on the stool again. This time I improved both the design and the process. The wax became 20 millimeters thick, the legs wider and the holes fewer. I performed the first molding in my bath, and once I had a seat surface and legs I moved to the kitchen sink. This is smaller than the bath, enabling all four corners of the sink to be used simultaneously, one for each leg. Once I had removed the stool from the sink, the process of carving the chamfer on all of the holes began again.

_____ This time instead of submerging the stool in hot water, I used a hot-air gun to smooth the surface of the wax before the stool was delivered to Morganic Metal. My wax stool was wired up with electrodes and fastened in a custom metal frame. Then it was sprayed with a special silver solution and submerged in the electro-deposition tank. Once sufficient deposition of nanocrystalline copper had occurred, the stool was removed from the tank. Gentle heat was applied to the base of the legs and the wax began to melt out, until all but a thin residue of wax lining the inner walls of the stool had been extracted. In theory, this residue was easily removable by submerging the stool in a tank of aqueous detergent for ultrasonic cleaning. In practice, this penultimate process proved catastrophic. Electrical faults are impossible to predict. A time switch above the cleaning tank caused an electrical fire and my almost-completed stool was released into the flames. At temperatures above 300 degrees copper distorts, wrinkles and blisters. Worse still, the nanocrystalline metal structure that had grown over sixty hours of electro-deposition became soft and malleable. Once again, all my labour was ruined. But I decided to attempt to salvage the burnt remains. The stool was sandblasted to remove the burnt plastic and a new copper layer was grown on it. The resultant stool has a highly irregular texture across the seat and two blistered legs. I decided not to tamper with these unintended details: they give the stool a character I could never have arrived at, and display the process so important to my work. No doubt about it: my copper stool is as it was meant to be.

_____ www.maxlamb.org
_____ www.rca.ac.uk
_____ Text: Max Lamb

Prior to the bath in hot water, British designer Max Lamb milled the holes on the top and bottom using a plain cutter.

Crystallized Message

For his Second Nature exhibition at the Design Center 21_21 Design Sight in Tokyo, Tokujin Yoshioka created a chair made of crystals, or to be more precise, fibres grown from polyester in a mineral solution. The crystallization process took one month to complete. The result appears confusingly artificial and natural at one and the same time. The chair is not particularly suitable for sitting on, it primarily makes a statement.

Here, the design is largely left to chance. Yoshioka grew his Venus Chair in a bath with a special mineral solution. Within a month, the textile, made of polyester fibers, had transformed itself into a unique crystal armchair.

_____ Tokujin Yoshioka is keeping the exact formula of the Venus Chair a secret. The 42-year-old Japanese designer will say only this: "One half of the production process is my doing; nature takes care of the rest. I immerse a soft fabric made of polyester fibers into a large tank containing a special mineral solution. Natural crystals then form on the fibers and they grow gradually until the Venus Chair is finished." Although the frame of the sponge-like fabric provides an outline of the shape, and although Yoshioka himself decides when the process is actually complete, the final shape is created by means of a process that is largely left to chance. Seen in this light, the Venus Chair is a piece of artificial nature.

_____ However, Yoshioka does not see any contradiction between artificiality and naturalness. He talks of "interplay between mankind and nature" and of the poetic message he aims to convey with the Venus Chair. Beauty is primarily to do with chance, "simply because chance lies outside our power of imagination". He calls the chair, in which he sees embodied the

image of the goddess of beauty, Venus, "a form created by nature, whose beauty we cannot comprehend". And it is precisely this natural beauty he wishes to draw attention to with the Venus Chair. "We live in an age in which almost anything is possible thanks to the rapid technological development, computer renderings etc." Bucking to this trend, with the Venus Chair Yoshioka aims to reveal by way of example that there can also be things which are created not just by technology, but also by nature. Products which initially defy the category of logic and thus touch us on an emotional level – be it negatively or positively.

_____ Yet the message of Yoshioka's chair is not just one of criticizing technology, it is also an ecological message. The Japanese designer hopes that his crystal chair will encourage people to focus on current ecological issues. Given the ongoing debate on climate change and its devastating consequences, there is a greater awareness of ecological problems, he says. But how could he make a personal contribution? "I am convinced that we can sensitize people to the environment simply by presenting them with the beauty of nature", says Yoshioka. Thus the Venus Chair is far more than a regular chair for sitting on. Otherwise, if the function of a product is very important to him, other aspects count in this case – he puts the crystal chair "somewhere between design and art". Is he intending to sell it, if possible, at a horrendous price as design art? "No", answers Yoshioka, "I just want as

Below: does starting with a soft material achieve the desired effect? Right page: polyester fiber textile in the various phases of crystallization.

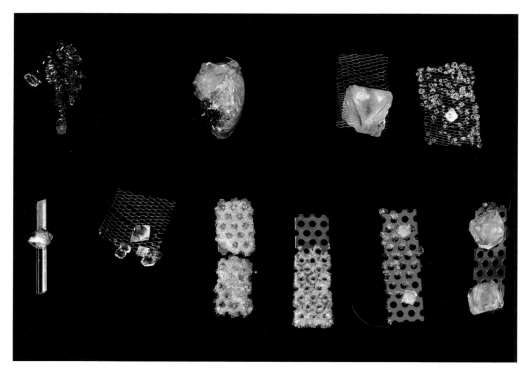

The Venus Chair expresses Tokujin Yoshioka's design philosophy: for him, beauty has much more to do with chance than with the latest technologies. Yoshioka is convinced that we need more emotional design.

many people as possible to see it and interact with it, ideally in public places, in Europe and the USA". It looks like this man is serious about his message.

_____ If we examine Yoshioka's design more closely, we quickly notice that all his work is based on a certain philosophy. The Japanese designer, who has had his own studio in Tokyo since 2000, and who works for companies that include Moroso, Driade, Hèrmes and Swarovski, rejects the classic, rational design concept, and instead calls for emotional design. "What we need is a new kind of emotion in design", he says, "from joy to an everyday, banal feeling of happiness. At the end of the day it is feelings that complete design." It is hardly surprising that Yoshioka does not set much store by exterior form. He even says, "insofar as it is possible, I do not wish to create a form". He primarily takes materials and technologies as his starting point. Many of his works stand out for their use of unconventional materials. One of his best-known pieces of furniture, Honey-pop (2001), is an armchair made of 120 sheets of glassine paper which, in order to sit on it, you have to pull apart like an accordion, and whose structure calls to mind, honeycomb. His Pane Chair made of polyester fibers is baked in a furnace. And his chair with the descriptive name "Chair that disappears in the rain" wins us over first and foremost with its ingenious material, namely, a special optical glass that makes the chair invisible in the rain. In 2003 Yoshioka did, in fact, exhibit the chair in the Roppongi Hills area of Tokyo. Wholly in keeping with his philosophy of emotional design, he loves it when people are able to respond directly to his work. Ever since he transformed the Moroso showroom at the Milan Furniture Fair 2007 into a poetic landscape made up of two million transparent straws, thus causing a sensation among the audience, people have expected extraordinary installations and spectacular orchestrations from him. Yoshioka himself believes that his products appeal primarily because he discovers a hidden beauty in things which others have not noticed hitherto. Perhaps this, too, is where the secret of the Venus Chair lies, for the crystallization process is in itself nothing new, but the context in which Yoshioka uses it certainly is.

_____ www.tokujin.com
_____ Text: Katharina Altemeier

Index

Imprint

Idea and Concept: Gerrit Terstiege

Project Management: Ramona Rockel, Gerrit Terstiege
Design and Layout: Silja van der Does, www.siljavanderdoes.com
Cover Photography: KGID, Munich
Typesetting: Silja van der Does, Amelie Solbrig
Text Editing: Markus Zehentbauer, Karen Bofinger
Translations: Jeremy Gaines, Frankfurt
Copy Editing: Susanne Dickel, Cologne
Production: Amelie Solbrig

Library of Congress Control Number: 2009928370

Bibliographic information published by the German National Library
The German National Library lists this publication in the Deutsche National-
bibliografie; deta...
http://dnb.d-nb.

This work is subje
whole or part of
lation, reprinting   ns-
duction on micro   )-
kind of use, perr   any

This book is also
(ISBN 978-3-0346

© 2009 Birkhäuse
Basel · Boston · E
P.O. Box 133, CH-
Part of Springer

Printed on acid-f
Printed in Germa

ISBN 978-3-0346

9 8 7 6 5 4 3 2 1

www.birkhauser.